# The Ernie O'Malley Story

## PADRAIC O'FARRELL

S0-AIT-484

**THE MERCIER PRESS**
DUBLIN and CORK

The Mercier Press Limited
4 Bridge Street, Cork
24 Lower Abbey Street, Dublin 1

© Padraic O'Farrell, 1983

ISBN 0 85342 692 9

For Cormac and Moira O'Malley,
Kaye Hogan and Eithne Golden Sax

Printed by Litho Press Co., Midleton, Co. Cork.

# Contents

# Acknowledgements

I wish to thank Ernie O'Malley's son, Cormac, for his generous assistance with this work. Also Ernie's sister, Kathleen, and his sister-in-law, Maura.

I am deeply grateful to Eithne Golden Sax for her meticulous, efficient and marvellously energetic research which contributed so much towards shaping part of this biography. Also her sister Deirdre and her brother Terence who kindly gave permission to quote from his writings.

I am indebted to many others for their assistance including the following: Kerry Holland, Seamus Helferty and University College Dublin Archives; Alf MacLochlann and the Staff of the National Library; the Under-Treasurer, Librarian and Staff, The King's Inns Library; Patrick Melvin, Oireachtas Library; Public Records Office; Comdt Peter Young and the Army Archives; Librarian and Staff, Longford-Westmeath Library; Michael O'Malley, County Manager, John O'Donnell, County Secretary, Mayo County Council, Staff members — May, Muriel and Clare; Carmel Gallagher, Western Health Board; Gyniver Jones, BBC Written Archives; Lord Walston; Lord Killanin; Sir Gilbert Laithwaite; Seán MacBride, S.C.; Dr C. S. (Todd) Andrews; Dr Cyril Cusack; Dr Bryan MacMahon; Kathleen Napoli McKenna; Brother W. P. Allen; Mary Clarke, Archivist, Dublin Corporation; James White, ex-Director, National Gallery; Liam O'Flaherty; Trinity College Library; Col James Croke; Col R. Bunworth; Sighle Bean Uí Dhonnchadha; Peadar O'Donnell; Noreen Moynihan, NUI; Marion O'Rahilly; Sean Dowling; Bill McKenna; Niall Casey; Spanish Embassy (Miss Slattery); Irish Consul, Barcelona; Seamus Kelly; Pan Collins; Maureen Potter; Ulick O'Connor; Patsy Harolds; Brigadier General Hartigan; John Raleigh; Greg Dunphy; Margaret Kidney, UCD Records Office; Professor Robert Dudley-Edwards; Col Dan Bryan; Capt John Carroll; Patrick Brennan; Frank McDonnell; Liam Egan, Castlebar Educational Centre; Jim Kemmy, Willie Gleeson, Anne Chambers. . . and a very patient family, with Niamh as chief proofreader.

# Introduction

Pondering a publisher's request for a biography of Ernie O'Malley, I happened upon the following statement from Dr C. S. (Todd) Andrews' autobiography, *Dublin Made Me:*

> I knew Ernie O'Malley very well. . . Of all the people I met and knew. . . he was the only one whom I would judge worthy of a full biography on a scale which would commend universal rather than merely Irish interest.

Then I recalled that while researching my *Who's Who in the Irish War of Independence 1916-1921* and subsequently *The Seán Mac Eoin Story* I had come across references to O'Malley, not just in one locale but here, there and everywhere across the land. An irreverent commentator might have labelled him a Paladin *(Have Gun, Will Travel)*, who was available wherever he was required throughout the War of Independence and the Civil War.

I was intrigued by what promised to be an enigmatic biographical study. However, I hesitated because exploits of persons who have become folk-heroes in battle might be inclined to foment revolutionary concepts or to encourage illegal brigandry among a people who ought now to be concerned with a new patriotism, not of the gun but of the spade and lathe. Chronicling events and personalities from the troubled period of our country's history is for me a humble service to that history. I attempt to present facts in a clear, unemotive manner, unbiased and fair.

I consider the Civil War to have been a major tragedy. Indeed, most of its veterans with whom I converse think similarly. In following my biography of Seán Mac Eoin by studying one of his opponents in that conflict, I trust that I underline the wish of a younger generation to look objectively on the event and shun divisions caused by it. I would also hope that it might be symbolic of a need to heal cancers within our society in a calm and sensible manner.

So much for an introduction to my reasoning, but what of

my subject?

Writing in a 1937 Christmas number of *The Kerryman* on the role of the National University in Ireland's fight for freedom, Francis Andrews included Pearse, McDonagh, Barry, Flood, Ryan and Darcy. Of O'Malley he said: 'It must be left to another generation to view in its proper perspective the influence which this "Man from God-knows-where" exerted on the movement throughout Ireland. . .'

I would consider it impertinent for one of my generation to judge people who helped lay the foundation stone of our state, but chronicling is not judgement. To record fairly is not to condemn nor approve.

The subject of this biography is, without doubt, a most complex figure in our country's history. Some of his surviving colleagues in two wars disliked him intensely. They labelled him 'a sham', 'a cod' who was 'always trying to impress'. Others spoke kindly of him, and offered excuses for his failings to which they too admitted. But *all* of them agreed that this man was a brave, courageous fighter who did not merely instruct and organise his men, but was ever in the van of the attack, displaying daring and bravery.

But to contemplate a biography of Ernie O'Malley on the strength of his involvement in Ireland's struggle for independence and her Civil War would be ridiculous. For here was a globe-trotting Gulliver whose interests in people and cultures brought him to Spain, France, Italy and the USA, to fraternise with Basques, Catalonians and Indians as well as with wealthy patrons of the arts.

Here was a writer regarded by *The Times* as being 'of high artistic and literary quality'. *On Another Man's Wound,* his book on the War of Independence, is still selling well, as is *Raids and Rallies* and *The Singing Flame,* his personal account of the Civil War prepared for publication by Frances-Mary Blake. His two large volumes tell about a man's exploits as experienced by himself, but I have, of course, used other sources as well, the more to consolidate O'Malley's prominence in those struggles: private papers of Michael Collins, Richard Mulcahy and others as well as O'Malley's own — some of which were captured with Ernie during the Civil War. School records, memorabilia, notebooks, diaries and assorted documents were perused. Dozens of O'Malley's relatives, colleagues and contemporaries were interviewed.

If the biography that emerges blemishes a national hero, that is unfortunate, but a biographer's duty is to discover and record facts about a person. If, in doing so, the myth suffers, might that not make the subject more praiseworthy? For myth is concerned with a supernatural person and a man is only an allegory if bereft of his humanity. Revealing humanity involves laying bare failings as well as fortitudes, and only by coming to terms with a person's bad points can we fully appreciate what is noble within him.

Tony Woods, an IRA staff captain who soldiered alongside Ernie O'Malley said of *The Singing Flame:* 'I read Frances-Mary Blake's book about him. It was no more a story of O'Malley; it was just adulation for a man which was not true. You would imagine there was no one else there. . .'*

Ernie O'Malley took the title of his first book from an old Irish proverb: 'It is easy to sleep on another man's wound.' In presenting his biography, I would like to dip into my own book of proverbs and sayings entitled *Gems of Irish Wisdom* by quoting:

'A questioning man is half-way to being wise.'
        and
'There's no wise man without some fault.'

* * *

* *Survivors*, Uinseann Mac Eoin, Argenta Publications.

# 1

# Beginnings and Early Manhood

*'Twas a proud and stately castle*
*In the years of long ago*
*When the dauntless Grace O'Malley*
*Ruled a queen in fair Mayo.*
*And from Bernham's lofty summit*
*To the waves of Galway Bay*
*And from Castlebar to Ballintra*
*Her unconquered flag held sway.*

The song 'Granuaile' is said to have been composed by the Mayo survivors of the battle of Ballinamuck, Co Longford. Franco-Irish forces had delivered a blow to England's insular security at Castlebar and had fought a gallant retrograde movement before their inland surrender on 8 September 1798, the Year of the French. There were threatened revolts and occasional skirmishes throughout the nineteenth century but Ireland did not again seek the arbitration of battle until Easter Week 1916.

The name of the song's sixteenth century queen had become a term of affection for this island. It still lingers, although the very real woman of considerable maritime prowess is remembered mainly by legend and by myth. Only her great fortresses remain to recall her might. Rockfleet Castle, a silent sentinel, frowns on Clew Bay's heavy lidded waters. On Clare Island, the name 'Grainne's Castle' is bestowed upon a heap of ruins. Even her last resting place is unknown. Burrishoole Abbey, which figures in this story, has been mentioned.

The O'Malley (Ó Máille) sept was one of the best known in north Connaught, yet it was in Mayo that the 'O' prefix was mostly discarded. There are found Maileys, Melias or simply Malleys throughout the county, whose centre of administration is Castlebar.

Nationalist traditions were not, however, pertinent at the wedding of a Castlebar man on 29 October 1894. On that day, Bernard Kearney's daughter Marion married Luke Malley's son Luke junior. The Kearneys were from Cloonroughan near Castlerea in Co Roscommon, but the wedding certificate gave Marion's address as 1 Melrose Avenue, Fairview, Dublin. Richard Healy and Maura Dobbin witnessed the ceremony performed by Canon William Keon, at Fairview Roman Catholic Church. The groom's occupation appeared as 'clerk to a solicitor'. Malachy Kelly was that lawyer, but the work involved officiating for the Congested Districts Board. (The board begot the Land Commission to which it handed over its functions in 1923.)

Luke Malley is remembered as a dignified gentleman, a citizen who respected law and order and demanded it in return. He supported the establishment and was well thought of by administrators in the town, by the police and by the clergy. Marion was a large, strong woman who aspired to achieving social status.

Luke and Marion lived in Ellison Street, Castlebar. Their first child, Frank was born on 19 October 1895 at a Dublin nursing home. Ernest Bernard followed on 26 May 1897. The first girl Marion, who was later to become known as 'Sweetie', saw the light of day just over a year later on 16 June 1898. Other children born while the parents lived in Mayo were Albert Patrick Victor, called Bertie, Cecil Patrick, Charles and John Patrick.

From an early age the Malley children addressed their father as 'Sir'. This was not unusual in well disciplined homes at the time. Mrs Malley taught them good manners. She was a methodical woman who instilled an admirable sense of respect in her children. She had a sense of propriety — and she stated that she came from, as she pronounced it 'Castleree'. It was not 'Castleray' for that town was in Antrim, she pointed out. Many would disagree with her, but not in the Malley home. There was an acceptance of parental authority there.

In the running of the home Marion was assisted by a lady sent by the master of the workhouse. She was accorded a more grandiose title of 'our nurse Nannie' by Ernie in his later writings. He grew up in an environment most unconducive to nurturing nationalistic emotions. His home in Ellison Street was opposite the barracks of the Royal Irish Constabulary and his parents were pleased to have the respect of that body who represented the front line of imperial power in Ireland. Again, this was not unusual, for the constabulary had an active relationship with the society for which it functioned. As a centralised, Castle-directed authority, it served as the chief government agency — not just in a police role, but in many administrative functions. Besides its practical importance it also presented a significant symbol for all who upheld the British administration as well as for those who opposed it.

While the Malley parents would have wished a protected childhood for their offsprings, they inevitably picked up some of the folklore of the countryside: 'Nannie's' stories of fairies, ghosts and banshees; tales from Celtic mythology or from *Ancient Legends of Ireland* just published then by 'Speranza' of *The Nation* — the indefatigable Lady Jane Francesca Wilde whose husband came from Marion Malley's own home town. But no latent interest was fired by the contact.

Dinner-table talk centred around Charles Stewart Parnell — but with never a word about Kitty O'Shea! The great political leader's concept of Home Rule survived him and John Redmond became leader of the re-united Parnellites in 1900. Perhaps they discussed the latest cinematography shown by the Protestant rector. Certainly, the first issue of the *United Irishman* or the formation of *Cumann na nGaedheal* or *Inghinidhe na hÉireann* were events of the turn of the century not alluded to, for young hearts were not to be exposed to any revolutionary suggestions by righteous parents. Again it must be stressed that this attitude was not uncommon in Irish towns. On the contrary, all law-abiding conformers behaved in much the same manner. Ernie Malley objected when he was first called by the Irish form of his name, Ó Máille. A close associate of his in later years recorded that he had no interest in the language or in Gaelic tradition. But can another judge a man's subconscious? Could a receptive, developing young mind have been fully insulated against the strength of the land about him: butter-women and farming folk in town on fair-day, some of them speaking in Irish; the tree in the Mall which had been the gallows for a priest of his own religion; pikeheads taken from the thatch and proudly displayed by the descendant of one who went to General Humbert's assistance in 1798; Killala, the 'Races of Castlbar', and his namesake Grace O'Malley who refused the title bestowed upon her by Elizabeth I whom she considered her equal? It is illogical to assume that the young Ernie avoided inculcation completely.

Malachy Kelly, Luke Malley's boss, had made a name for himself when he was admitted as a solicitor in 1871 at 21 years of age. He was appointed Sessional Crown Solicitor for Mayo in 1881 and Crown Solicitor in 1884. He married the daughter of Sir Patrick Coll. On 9 December 1905, the *Irish Law Times* reported:

> Sir Patrick Coll KCB has retired on pension under the age limit and his office has been divided into two departments. Mr Malachy J. Kelly has been promoted from the Crown Solicitorship for the County of Mayo to the one under the designation of Chief Crown Solicitor for Ireland, with offices at the Castle, and Mr William M. Lane, Assistant Solicitor, Board of Works, has been promoted to the other, under the designation of Treasury Solicitor in Ireland.

Malachy Kelly moved to Dublin to take up his new and exalted position. Luke Malley followed within the year and was soon installed as clerk, first grade, at the headquarters of the Congested Districts Board at Rutland Square.

On moving to Dublin, Luke Malley set up house at 120 Drumcondra Road, moving later to 'St Kevin's', Iona Drive, Glasnevin. Luke Kevin was the first Dublin-born child. He arrived on 10 January 1907. When Kathleen Mary followed a long line of boys her father got drunk for the first time in his life, according to his wife. That was on 11 May 1910. Two more boys completed the large family of eleven — Brendan Joseph (28 March 1912) and Desmond (12 March 1918) — so there were still babies in the home when Ernie was a fully fledged revolutionary.

## School and University

At O'Connell School in North Richmond Street, Dublin, there is a room commemorating a reception into the order of the Irish Christian Brothers. It is the place where dramatist, novelist and poet Gerald Griffin received his habit in 1838. The grandfather clock by which he checked the time still strikes the hour for the community there. A fine museum has on display the only known complete set of ration cards for the 1847 Famine Soup Kitchens. It contains memorabilia of famous past pupils, including Kevin Barry and Frank Flood — another executed student never accorded the same prominence as Barry.

About the time Arthur Griffith was launching the first issue of *Sinn Féin*, Ernie Malley began to attend O'Connell School. He is remembered as 'a tousled, flaming red-head with a scar on his upper lip from broken glass, who never stayed long before a mirror'. 'Red Mick' they called him. He settled well into his studies and passed his preparatory grade examination under the Intermediate Board System in 1911. About 11,000 Irish pupils sat for this examination each year. It catered for the middle and lower-middle classes by preparing them for commercial and civil service positions or for university studies. He passed junior grade in June 1912, a few months before the issuing and signing of the Ulster Covenant by Edward Carson and others. By the time he reached middle grade he had thrown a duster at a teacher and had joined the set referred to by the community as the 'Full Backs'. These students were not very industrious, but sat back — fully!

He began to show an interest in girls and to slip away to an occasional dance. Some O'Connell boys 'mitched' from school on Thursdays, when the Dublin cattle market was held. Lads assisting drovers in bringing livestock from the North Circular Road to the docks would earn five or ten shillings. Ernie was reported unofficially to have participated along with Emmet Dalton. Both of these pupils sat their middle grade examinations unsuccessfully in June 1913. (Dalton's examination number was 5384, Malley's 6131.)

In senior grade, Class Number Eleven was the 'pass class who usually failed' according to an old teacher. Its students had not passed middle grade and there was no reason to expect better results at end-of-year, which was also the end of their secondary schooling. During his first term in senior grade things were happening outside the school which were to affect the course of young Malley's life. He was still sheltered from their significance, however, by a protective and un-nationalistic home environment.

In October 1913 James Connolly formed the Citizen Army after James Larkin had been jailed for his 'criminal syndicalism' as the court called his actions on behalf of the workers. On 25 November the Irish Volunteers were formed. Contemporaries of Ernie in O'Connell School were to figure with him in this and other spheres: Gabriel Fallon, William Staines, Noel Lemass.

The Malley brothers Patrick, Cecil and Charlie received schooling at O'Connell's too. Charlie carried on a small illicit trade in the sale of copy books. His parents heard about it, felt it was a reflection on the family's good name and removed him from the school. None of the organisational ability which made itself apparent in his later life showed at this stage of Ernie's life. An 'O'Malley Gang' is recalled by a schoolmate, however, so his leadership qualities may have been emerging. His use of the 'O' prefix seems to date from about that time too. Only himself and Desmond used it constantly. Indeed birth registrations affix the letter to Desmond alone.

Ernie failed his senior grade examination in June 1914 and he left O'Connell School. On 6 July 1915 he was among 45 candidates who sat for Dublin Corporation Scholarships in connection with the National University of Ireland. He was among the 24 to whom the Right Honourable Lord Mayor and Burgesses granted scholarships. In the autumn of 1915, over a year after leaving secondary school, he entered University College Dublin to study medicine.

Arms had been landed at Howth for the Volunteers (July 1914) and in the following September John Redmond advocated enlistment of Irishmen in the British army to fight in the Great War. This caused a split in the Volunteer movement with Eoin MacNeill leading the minority in opposing enlistment. During 1915 the Irish Republican Brotherhood (IRB) Military Council was appointed, as publications like *Éire, Workers Republic* and *Nationality* appeared and whipped up the breezes of nationalism.

Ernie's schoolmate Emmet Dalton joined the British army, as did the eldest Malley brother Frank. In university there were people like Joe Sweeney and Patrick Magilligan to influence Ernie, although he said himself, 'There one heard little of the Volunteers or the various other movements.'

The struggle for independence began on Easter Monday, 24 April 1916. Ernie O'Malley had an early meeting with a victim of the fighting as he sat with other students on the steps of the National Library. Approaching this habitual haunt of college lads there came an injured British soldier, seeking assistance. Ernie directed him 'inside, downstairs on the left' to the ladies' toilet, but these high spirits belied an anxiety brought about by his incomprehension of what was going on. He almost found himself defending Trinity College on the invitation of a member of the Officer Training Corps there.

As it turned out, he fired his first shots from a rifle before the week had ended — in a type of an independent action by himself and a friend who secured the use of a weapon. He had come down on the side of the insurgents. By the time the rebellion ended five days after it began, O'Malley was fully in sympathy with Pearse's sentiments. When Pearse and his companions were executed in May he became a confirmed revolutionary. He was particularly upset at the execution of Major John MacBride, who, as he said, 'had been kind to us as children'.

He still kept his activities from his parents, but the Volunteers began taking up more of his time than his studies. His membership of F Company of the First Dublin Battalion involved him in routine church-gate collections as well as assorted drilling, route-marching and recruitment within the university. He also helped along the fortunes of a Fianna Éireann youth company of which some of his younger brothers became members. His superiors included Paddy Holohan who had participated in the attempt to blow up the Magazine Fort in the Phoenix Park on the morning of Easter Monday 1916 and later fought on the North Quays and Brunswick Street; Liam Archer, a civil servant held by the Volunteeers in the GPO and later one of their fervent organisers, and Diarmuid O'Hegarty were officers in his battalion too. Frank McCabe was his company commander.

He began to meet with people who had been imprisoned for their revolutionary activities. He drilled with broom handles alongside working men, unemployed fathers of families as well as academics, literary and artistic people. He paid a few pence each week towards the purchase of a weapon. When he received it, he hid it beneath the floorboards in his room.

His streak of daring became manifest when his brother was home on leave from the Great War, having been wounded. He dressed in Frank's uniform in order to purchase a weapon, revolver and ammunition. On being informed that he needed a permit he boldly took himself off to the Provost Marshal's office in Dublin Castle to obtain one. On another occasion he was aided by a colleague in upending a member of the Dublin Metropolitan Police during a baton-charge. He ran away with the constable's baton.

Ernie O'Malley spent more time in the Gaelic League drill-hall than in UCD study-hall, yet he passed his first medical examination in the fall of 1916. Although a member of the Gaelic League, he had no fanatical love of the language so prevalent among his colleagues. Indeed, he stoutly defended the English if he heard them spoken of unjustly. He disliked coarse language and uncouth manners.

He participated in the normal student practices of dancing — even *ceili*-going. He lounged in St Stephen's Green or drank coffee in Bewley's of Grafton Street. He became involved in drama and had associations with an amateur group called the Rainbow Chasers. He read the works of former Irish patriots, but not many medical books. He failed his second medical examination in 1917, and by repeating that failure the following March, he lost his scholarship. Thomas Ashe was dying after his hunger strike during Ernie's first sitting. During his second attempt, there was a large scale hunger strike in Mountjoy, Dundalk and Cork. Then followed John Redmond's death, shortly after his call to draft a constitution for Ireland within the British empire. Lloyd George announced conscription for Ireland early in April and there followed a conference at the Mansion House. The so-called 'National Cabinet' was comprised of Dillon and Devlin of the Parliamentary Party, Griffith and de Valera of Sinn Féin, Labour's William O'Brien and his namesake of the 'All for Ireland League', T. M. Healy and others. It pledged to deny the right of the British government to enforce compulsory service in Ireland and to resist attempts at conscription by the most effective means at its disposal.

Ernie O'Malley participated in the spectacular funeral for Ashe and defied threats against it. If he did engage in 'stock rustling' during his days in O'Connell School, it stood him in good stead when, as controller of food for Sinn Féin, Diarmuid Lynch organised the seizing of pigs bound for England. Ernie was one of the First Battalion members who herded the animals for slaughter and who 'brought home the bacon' on pointed sticks to Donnelly's factory from where it was distributed throughout the country. O'Malley's romanticism would have relished the ploy whereby Lynch got married while in prison for this misdemeanour.

He may not have been in form for enjoying any situation, however, for his secret was out at his home and things became intolerable. His point of view was ruled out of order. He had little option but to 'break' from the family which supported the establishment and thought more of their son in the British army. He left home for good in March 1918. This particular action parries the harsh verdict passed by a prominent member of the IRA who later fought alongside Ernie and who claimed that O'Malley had no political convictions whatsoever, but that his involvement in the struggle was quite accidental.

Now a full-time NCO in the IRA, a member of the IRB and with no further ties, Ernie answered a call to volunteer for staff work and was detailed to report to Richard (Dick) Mulcahy in Dungannon. Mulcahy gave him command of Coalisland with the rank of second lieutenant. His inexperience was made up for by enthusiasm and by sound advice from Peadar O'Donnell and Simon Donnelly.

Soon he was back in Dublin, however, this time reporting to the director of organisation Michael Collins. Collins called him Earnán and despatched him to Offaly to organise a brigade there. He furnished him with documentation on methods of organisation, billeting and rationing. Ernie O'Malley was now a GHQ staff officer. Leslie Price (who later married Tom Barry) accompanied Ernie to Offaly to organise Cumann na mBan there.

Offaly had the distinction of anticipating the Easter Week rebellion. RIC Sergeant Philip Ahearn raided a Sinn Féin meeting in William Street, Tullamore on 20 March 1916 and was fired upon and injured. Tullamore's local hero Peadar Bracken fought in O'Connell Street and Seamus O'Brennan in the GPO, while Seamus Kelly was in action at Ashbourne. Other Offalymen had been active too, and they boasted in song:

> The fight began in Tullamore
> When men refused to bend
> Their knees to Castle bullies,
> But defied them to the end.

> Bold patriots from this sturdy place
> Were fighting all around,
> In the thickest of the Dublin fray
> Some of these men were found.
>
> And when heroes bold from Lusk
> By Ashe were led along
> A Tullamore man's rifle
> Was cracking in the throng. . .

To put it bluntly, these men resented the comparatively inexperienced O'Malley coming to teach them how to organise. They claimed that he did little but march the Cumann na mBan women from Tullamore to Clara, a distance of seven miles. Yet there is evidence of their disapproving his rousing of Volunteers at night and marching them across country, through streams and marshes. Such training would not be appreciated as being important to build up stamina and resistance.

The meticulous officer began to emerge in Offaly. A field notebook bore messages to O/C Offaly Brigade with implicit instructions to keep a duplicate of the correspondence, to write clearly when replying and to print all names of places. O'Malley was obviously studying his staff duties manual. An example of his impetuosity appeared in Message No. 18 dated 14 May 1918. It requested a sheath for a knife 'as soon as possible. I want it in an hour's time as I must leave TULLAMORE. . .' There were detailed instructions about a band of leather to prevent the hand slipping and another to attach it to a belt. A diagram of the required leatherwork was included — and the signature was Earnán Ó Máille. There were also chop by chop accounts of how to cut sticks for bayonet drill!

Ernie met Austin Stack and Darrell Figgis in Tullamore, saying of the latter that he had an unfortunate habit of making enemies. Ernie himself did not make many friends, but perhaps this was because of the countryman's suspicion and dislike of outsiders interfering in their affairs. It was in Tullamore that he met for the first time a man for whom he had profound respect — Eamon de Valera.

Offaly people are keen, industrious, staunch and respectful (not for nothing did they earn the name the 'Faithful County'), but they are shrewd too and they accept little without questioning. They co-operated with this live-wire from GHQ, but they also whispered queries about his true identity. Who sent him? Why did he always escape detection when others carrying out his orders were being arrested. Even when the *bona fides* of the 'GHQ officer' were established to their satisfaction they disliked his zeal-ous pace. Toting his revolver, map case and perhaps binoculars also, he sped from town to town calling parades, outwitting the RIC, lecturing, demonstrating rifle-marksmanship and supervising the manufacture of simple explosives.

O'Malley is said to have left Offaly in disgust; there were no broken Volunteer hearts in the 'Green Fields Round Ferbane' at his departure.

Through Athlone and on to Roscommon moved the red-haired human dynamo. He realised the feelings of the country leaders but had little time to bother about them. There was a job to be done. He had studied the book. He would do it his way.

A Roscommon county councillor Michael Brennan from Carrickteel and his brother Jack, the Shouldice brothers and about twenty others had been imprisoned for their part in the Easter Week fighting in Dublin. One of these was Paddy Moran who was later to figure in Ernie O'Malley's jail escape (see p. 40). Ernie's mother was Roscommon born and Éamonn Ceannt was the son of an RIC sergeant stationed at Ballymoe — a barracks soon to feature in O'Malley's story. Fr Michael O'Flanagan was another pro-minent Roscommon man in Sinn Féin.

It has been said that the ballot boxes of the north Ros-common by-election of 1917 represented the reply of the Irish people to the post-Easter Week executions. George Noble Count Plunkett, father of the executed leader Joseph Mary, headed the poll in a consituency where three-quarters of the electorate were peasant proprietors who had benefited under various Land Purchase Acts of the establishment. Yet they returned the Sinn Féin supported abstentionist candidate. Feelings were high in Roscommon at the time of O'Malley's arrival. Count Plunkett had been arrested and deported. He was one of the many so treated because of alleged but unsubstantiated treasonable communication between Irishmen and Germans, the infamous 'German Plot'.

Some Roscommon folk cast cynical comment on the state of the Volunteers in the area about that time. They claimed that strengths had been extremely low before the threat of conscription but had jumped tenfold after Lloyd George's announcement. When the danger of conscription had passed, strengths dwindled again.

O'Malley had little time for parochial murmurings. He got on with the job of drilling with five foot poles, with organising raids for shotguns, revolvers and assorted weapons. He gave hints on how to remove shot from cartridges and replace it with slugs made from pieces of lead. The RIC marked him as a wanted man.

Statements have often been made to the effect that Ernie O'Malley held a healthy respect for human life and never fired first. One evening near Toberbride (Ballintober) he addressed Volunteers under the watchful gaze of an RIC sergeant and his constable. Later that night when his bicycle gave trouble at Ballymoe the same sergeant arrived and presented him with a warrant for his arrest. Ernie was first to have a revolver drawn and the sergeant challenged him to fire. He did not respond, even when the sergeant fired and hit him and police reinforcements arrived. With neck, left wrist and right ankle wounded he dashed from the village and fumbled through hedges and ditches, shaking off his pursuers. He dressed his wounds and bedded down for the night in the open air on the unfamiliar Galway side of the River Suck. At dawn, he swam to the Roscommon side again as a dragnet of RIC combed the Galway countryside for the elusive O'Malley. His wounds were dressed in a friendly house and he left the area on a borrowed bicycle.

Arthur Griffith had been elected an MP for East Cavan and the first post-1916 issue of *An tÓglach* was published on 15 August 1918 when O'Malley was again called to Michael Collins' headquarters. He was invited to proceed to London to transact some IRB business. This would involve adopting the guise of a British army officer, unarmed and open to the consequences of being arrested. His mission was secret but he appeared to enjoy it, especially saluting senior British officers and the like. In Liverpool he met Cathal Brugha who was over making an estimate for his notorious plan by which he intended shooting down each member of the British cabinet. (Seán Mac Eoin was to have been involved until Collins dismissed the idea.) O'Malley bought weapons and ammunition in small quantities before returning to Dublin.

The Third Annual Sinn Féin Conference was in progress when he reported back to Collins and received his next assignment.

Joe Sweeney commanded the Volunteers in west Donegal. He, Joe Doherty and Joe Ward were preparing to run in the general election in December. Some organisation was urgently needed. Adopting the names of Dowling, Gallagher and Kelly, Ernie went about his task with fervour. He soon became depressed, however, and despaired of getting anything done. He wondered if he possessed any organisational skill, if he was driving his men too hard — and he caught on to the craftiness of Donegal folk when he discovered himself inspecting the same faces in a number of companies. He consoled himself by putting it down to a desire to please the 'GHQ officer' with numbers, but he criticised an apparent lack of leadership too.

It has to be asked if perhaps O'Malley aggravated difficulties by attempting to impose regular army standards as absorbed by him from manuals. After all, Joe Sweeney had participated in the Easter Week Rebellion and had come under the attention of Head Constable Igoe, later leader of the notorious 'Igoe Gang' of provincial RIC brought to Dublin to identify IRA members. That was when Joe, while studying engineering at Galway University, was also instructing students in grenade assembly. He threw up his studies and returned to Donegal to prepare the Volunteers there. Then there were people like Dinny Houston who led a daring rescue, Jim McMonagle and Barney O'Donnell. Also, of course, Joe Doherty commanded north Donegal while Sam O'Flaherty straddled the Donegal–Derry border with his East Donegal Brigade. Joe Sweeney, later major general, may have come close to assessing O'Malley in his terse statement: 'A dedicated man, he had little patience for political affairs and, as the Volunteers were the backbone of the Sinn Féin clubs and were organising my compaign, he found it difficult to get them to meet to suit his arrangements.' As they say in Donegal, 'There's a power of meaning in the butt of that!'

# 2
# War of Independence

*She had strongholds on the headlands*
*And brave galleys on the sea*
*And no warlike chief or viking*
*E'er had bolder heart than she.*
*She unfurled her country's banner*
*High o'er battlement and mast*
*And 'gainst all the might of England*
*Kept it flying 'til the last.*

Dáil Éireann met for the first time in the Mansion House, Dublin, on 21 January 1919. Seventy-three Sinn Féin candidates who like Joe Sweeney had contested the election in December 1918 had been successful and refused to take their seats in the British parliament. Because of imprisonment and other reasons only twenty-seven were in attendance at the Mansion House to adopt a provisional constitution and declaration of independence. On the same day, at Soloheadbeg, Co Tipperary, a gelignite patrol was ambushed by Dan Breen and others and two policemen were killed. The War of Independence had started.

The intrepid Staff Captain O'Malley (for he had been promoted) was summoned from Donegal and ordered to head for Clare. A delicate situation had arisen there when the Brennan brothers resented a GHQ directive to form three independent brigades: East Clare, West Clare and Mid-Clare. They would have preferred divisional control of these units.

Clare had been an active area during the Land War — an event never given its due place in Irish history. Here again its people did not come up to O'Malley's expectations in filing reports, in attending lectures, in drilling. As he said, after hard work all day on their farms or in town they found it 'cruel hard to study'. However, like many another before and since, Ernie became spellbound by Clare's marvellous people, its fascinating folkways, the lively lilt of its music. A near-total rejection of proper military methods, of ceremonial trappings, of intelligence collection left him frustrated. All the more because he loved the perpetrators! They welcomed him to Clare and provided him with the best accommodation available; he chided them for thinking of creature comforts for him rather than looking after the organisation of the Volunteers.

Near Ennis, Ernie O'Malley again showed his reluctance to kill on one occasion when an RIC patrol was completely at the mercy of himself and two Volunteers. 'There was no moral element in my thoughts,' he said. He merely felt that 'shooting did not seem fair'. He found himself unable to convey his reasons to his disappointed subordinates.

Clare had been jubilant since de Valera's escape from Lincoln prison in February, but Ernie was despondent for he had become involved in a shooting incident against the RIC which resulted in widespread arrests. The police circulated the rumour that he was a spy and had deliberately missed the sergeant at whom he shot. After a meeting with Dick Mulcahy in Limerick, Ernie moved, at his behest, to north Tipperary. He met Dan Breen for the first time then, as well as the famous athlete Frank McGrath and 'Widger' Maher.

Shortly, however, Collins sent him back to Donegal with a new Webley ·45 revolver and an ultimatum to locate and capture 200 Ulster Volunteer rifles, 'and for Christ's sake, Earnán learn to shoot straight or I'll lose you one of these days,' added Michael. No rifles materialised and Ernie returned to paperwork at GHQ even as de Valera was departing for the USA to help raise funds for the new Dáil Loan.

It was during this period that Ernie got his greatest insight into Collins' intelligence system, into cross-channel operations and jail-escape plans. He worried because GHQ kept two complete lists of officers, down to company level, which could have been of enormous benefit to the British, if they were ever seized.

He also studied the men who led the movement. At that time Collins could drink, swear or fight; he could be jovial or depressed. He made an impact on his subordinates — but O'Malley liked neither his uncouth manner ('as judged by my early standards') nor his impish needling of certain officers. Mulcahy was extremely popular with the ladies of Cumann na mBan for his charming manner. He did not swear, drink nor smoke; he interrogated callers with a penetrating technique. Brugha too was abstemious while Diarmuid O'Hegarty struck him as being of even temperament, a good worker but a poor dresser! He listened to Ernie's suggestions politely but did not adopt many of them. Yet Ernie still admired his 'type of quick intellect'. O'Malley liked Gearóid O'Sullivan's decorum and his adroitness, but objected, as he did with Collins, to his treating rural officers in a smart fashion when they called. He thought O'Sullivan 'a pale reflection of Mick Collins'.

Perhaps O'Malley's presence at GHQ influenced Collins to quit smoking and drinking about that time. Or was he feeling the awesome responsibility of the Oath of Allegiance adopted by Dáil Éireann on 26 August, less than a month before the assembly was declared an illegal organisation? Already, the popular designation 'Irish Republican Army' was evolving, although the term was never suggested officially nor adopted by any deliberate policy. A new form of oath had been drawn up for Volunteers but Collins was furious when he discovered that O'Malley was administering it to north Dublin recruits before its ratification.

The campaign against the military and RIC was being stepped up, the latter considered as legitimate targets because of their being an extension of the British armed forces. They acted as intelligence agents in town and village and their barracks were defended in the fashion of military posts.

On 19 December 1919, Lord John Denton Pinkstone French, Lord Lieutenant of Ireland, was ambushed at

Ashtown but escaped injury. On 23 December the *Irish Bulletin* pointed out that in 1917 there were 719 acts of aggression against the Irish people but in the last six weeks of 1919 there were 3,187. These included 2,829 militaristic raids on private houses, 162 arrests, 126 sentences of imprisonment by paid magistrates.

On 30 December it gave a table under the heading:

### HOW TO RESTORE LAW AND ORDER

|                               | 1917 | 1918  | 1919   |
| ----------------------------- | ---- | ----- | ------ |
| Military murders              | 7    | 6     | 7      |
| Deportations                  | 24   | 91    | 22     |
| Armed assaults on civilians   | 18   | 81    | 382    |
| Raids on private houses       | 11   | 260   | 12,589 |
| Arrests                       | 349  | 1,107 | 963    |
| Courts martial                | 36   | 62    | 259    |
| Sentences                     | 269  | 973   | 778    |
| Proclamations & suppressions  | 2    | 32    | 364    |
| Suppression of newspapers     | 3    | 12    | 26     |
|                               | 719  | 2,624 | 15,390 |

Guerrilla warfare is considered to be a difficult and strange type of fighting. It takes great courage and its participants endure the moral distinction drawn between men who kill in uniform and those who wear plain clothes for the purpose. The 1920s were ushered in by typical guerrilla actions at Drumbane, Araglen, Baltinglass, Aghern and Holycross. A hunger strike began in Cork prison on 6 January 1920.

The Dáil Loan Fund was opened in New York and the Home Rule Bill was introduced in the House of Commons again.

The Bill was Lloyd George's reaction to the developing reign of terror in Ireland and was typical of British reaction to Irish violence since Gladstone: a combination of redress and coercion. It proposed setting up two parliaments, one for the north-eastern counties and another for the remaining twenty-six, both having limited powers. Its dire consequences were not appreciated by Sinn Féin who chose to ignore it.

Meanwhile Ernie O'Malley was in Monaghan pursuing his organisational duties. The county of the wee hills had experienced little fighting and its nationalist population included old Nationalist party and Ancient Order of Hibernian elements. These were somewhat hostile to Sinn Féin. There was no brigade structure in the county when, in 1919, Diarmuid O'Hegarty drew up a national IRA organisation. Independent battalion organisations existed. These were based mainly on Sinn Féin clubs. Ernie encouraged regular meetings and some positive activity. He conducted training sessions and instituted intelligence collection agencies.

He had quite remarkable ideas about psychology. On one occasion he strapped two guns to his hips while he accompanied a local leader down the main street of a market town. He assumed this would boost the man's spirits. 'It's good for morale,' he explained. The droll Monaghan man replied, 'It might be good for yours, but not for mine.'

It was decided that Monaghan's initial action should be against the RIC barracks at Shantonagh, Bellatrain or Ballytrain. Although boasting three forms of address the place was extremely isolated. The barracks was a semi-detached, two storey building commanding the Cootehill–Carrickmacross and Shercock–Castleblaney roads.

A tradesman Volunteer, Barney Marron of Ardragh, was carrying out repairs to the station and discovered that there were sufficient arms in the barracks to make the raid worthwhile. About 125 Volunteers were involved in the action. Many were merely standing by to precipitate road-blocks in the event of reinforcements arriving to relieve the garrison. Others were used simply to get as many as possible involved in this first challenge to the enemy. About thirty shotguns and as many conventional weapons were available to the Volunteers.

Eoin O'Duffy of Castleblaney, the local brigade commander, was the Ulster member of the Supreme Council of the IRB. Some reports say he and O'Malley jointly led the attack which began when, during the first moments of 14 February 1920, the residence facing the barracks was occupied by about thirty men. Other parties were led by P. J. O'Daly, Dan Hogan, Phil Marron, John McCann, Seamus McKenna, Charlie Emerson, Terry Magee and James Flynn.

The most detailed documentation of the event suggests that the owner of the occupied house, David Mitchell, had a store in the premises adjoining the barracks. This house shared the same roof with the barracks where Sergeants Graham and Lawton commanded four constables. While sporadic bursts of fire were exchanged between the barracks and the house opposite, the important Volunteer business was taking place in Mitchell's store. Pat McCabe, Tom and John Donnelly and Pat MacDonnell were setting gelignite to blast the wall of the barracks. Soon after 1 a.m. all was ready.

O'Duffy used a megaphone to call on the RIC to surrender. They refused to comply so he warned them of the prepared explosives. They still held fast. The gelignite was then detonated and O'Duffy once more demanded surrender. The police handed their weapons out through a window and then, covered by the dust of the explosion, they gave themselves up. Some were slightly wounded.

Lawton had been a tough sergeant so he feared severe reprisals. But the six carbines, a Verey light pistol, some ammunition and miscellaneous equipment were more important to his attackers who fled into the night with their booty. The time was nearing 4 a.m.

The barracks was badly damaged and at first light the mesmerised garrison sent Sergeant Graham to report the incident to their Carrickmacross headquarters.

Exaggerated reports about the Ballytrain attack circulated. They did little harm but they did make nationalists more sympathetic towards Sinn Féin, thus providing an impetus for recruitment. This was further stimulated when Eoin O'Duffy was arrested and lodged in Crumlin Road prison. Others involved in planning the attack were also arrested.

The RIC began to withdraw from their small rural posts and to adopt a siege situation in larger towns. The psychological effect of this on IRA volunteers was far more significant than the comparatively minor success at Ballytrain. This was precisely what O'Malley had hoped for. Where sympathy lay was underlined by a note from District Inspector Maunsell in Carrickmacross to the accountant-general's office. It accompanied a bill from the doctor who had been called to attend to the police wounded at Ballytrain. It recommended payment of the account 'because doctors do not care to have anything to do with policemen in these times'.

It was not until O'Duffy was released as a result of a hunger strike, however, that Monaghan Volunteers became really active. He and his colleagues had spent their imprisonment fruitfully drawing up plans for the development of the movement. Yet no British solider, Auxiliary or RIC member was killed there during the War of Independence. Three Black and Tans were shot later and the IRA lost a few men.

An account of the Ballytrain fight in the *Capuchin Annual* of 1970 bore no mention of Ernie O'Malley. In his book *On Another Man's Wound,* O'Malley, normally effusive, dismissed the event in half a dozen lines, saying merely that he was there. Could this be of significance to the rumour sometimes quoted that O'Malley abandoned the final stages of the Ballytrain attack to O'Duffy and Hogan?

On 6 March, Pierce McCan TD died in Gloucester jail, and on the 19th Thomas MacCurtain, the Lord Mayor of Cork, was shot dead in his home. Soon afterwards the Lord Mayor of Limerick Michael O'Callaghan and other prominent figures received threatening letters. On 22 March, the *Irish Times* said:

> . . . That the chief citizen of one of our great cities should be shot dead in his own house and that his murderers should escape, provide a terrible commentary on the state of this unhappy island.

The island's lot was to worsen. Three days afterwards, the first contingent of the Black and Tans arrived.

Ernie O'Malley's work continued. Despite the drawbacks, being a 'runner' — an outsider in a small community — carried certain advantages. A local organiser, however diplomatic or tactful, eventually becomes bogged down in petty jealousies and in personality clashes — legacies of generations of introverted parochialism in provincial Ireland. An emissary from without, however, is given due hearing and he also has the advantage of being able to act in accordance with his candid assessment of the situation as he finds it, without fear or favour towards local frictions — of which he is probably unaware anyhow.

Maintaining this aloofness is a lonely mission, however. Ernie O'Malley seldom joined in the fireside chat, in the card-games or singing as the *leac-na-teine* rattled to the tapping feet of the householders. If he had the use of a room he retired there to study military manuals and literature. The gaiety in the kitchen became but a distraction to the keen student of tactics, of leadership, of map-reading and musketry. Then again, what he absorbed — the theoretical warfare and written regulation — was not always acceptable to those whom he instructed.

Ostensibly, local commanders at first agreed with his suggestions, but this was often out of respect only. When he was gone on his way they frequently scorned his advice and continued operating in accordance with their own judgement, but that was to change.

The Black and Tans were beginning to make their presence felt and consequently battalion and brigade commanders became more amenable to acting on the recommendation of a learned advisor. Yet they maintained their traditional system of electing commanding officers. Here was a recurrence of the old Brehon system where tribal groupings operated under chosen leaders, but it was often faulty in a twentieth century society. The first proposal was invariably accepted by the general body who might know him to be completely unsuitable for the office. To oppose would be to cause ill-will.

Then there were military necessities which were completely incompatible with the Irish temperament. Punctuality, discipline and deportment were unacceptable impositions, methodology was alien.

After a spell of about three months in the field, O'Malley would report to headquarters and follow with a short break. He was then a slightly built man of about five feet ten inches, his crop of red hair accentuated by a red moustache. He found food and shelter in the houses of friends and at Scoil Íde. He still did not return home to Glasnevin where there was now a new infant brother of two. His many pouches, pockets and straps held his personal effects, all of which he transported on his bicycle. He felt his baggy trousers (which had belonged to a much larger man) and high boots looked odd in the city.

Early April saw the widespread burnings of income-tax offices and vacant RIC barracks by the IRA, the appointment of Sir Hamar Greenwood as chief secretary for Ireland and another hunger strike in Mountjoy. Eighty prisoners began the fast on 5 April. That day London's *Daily Herald* pronounced:

> There can no longer be any doubt that, in the eyes of the British government, Ireland is a foreign country to be governed after the fashion of a conquered and mandated province.

Lord French screamed of the IRA having an army of 100,000 'properly organised in regiments and brigades, led by disciplined officers'. Ernie O'Malley must have smiled.

There were numerous RIC deaths and an All-Ireland general strike ended when, after ten days of their fast, the Mountjoy political prisoners were released unconditionally.

Seán Treacy and Séamus Robinson, two Tipperary stalwarts, prevailed upon Michael Collins to send Ernie to their area. Desmond Ryan quoted Treacy as saying they 'had worn Collins down' despite Michael's intention to post O'Malley to Kerry.

So it was that Ernie O'Malley joyfully headed for the heart of the action — to the celebrated South Tipperary

Brigade area commanded by Robinson with Seán Treacy as vice-commandant. Here were men eager to learn but un-accustomed to handling weapons or to the rigours of tactics or other military training. Again the authoritarian aspect of leadership rested uneasily on a neighbourly people.

Men from four Tipperary battalions and from the East Limerick Brigade were marshalled for the attack on Holly-ford Barracks in May, led by O'Malley and Robinson. There was little available in the line of equipment: thirteen rifles with twenty rounds each, some hand grenades and explosives and a few handguns. Seán Treacy led a vigorous frontal attack firing from behind a low wall opposite the two storey building. As this softened up the besieged garri-son, O'Malley inspected outposts, aggravating some, en-couraging others and taking a little advice himself from Jim Gorman who had seen service in the First World War.

Then he and Robinson showed their true grit. Armed with two revolvers, grenades, detonators and hammers, their backs bent under the weight of cans of petrol and sods of paraffin-soaked turf, they shined up two ladders, battered in the slated roof and set the roof timbers ablaze with their merchandise.

Jim Gorman joined the pair and more petrol was splashed about and ignited as desperate rifle-fire sprang from the beleaguered RIC force within. O'Malley clung to the burning hot slates and engaged police who were firing from a lean-to attached to the main building. Gorman and Robinson fetched more petrol as Ernie kept their progress covered. He dropped one grenade accidentally just as Robinson was climbing up. Both men clung to their pre-carious perches and survived the blast which temporarily deafened Robinson. The fire from the outhouse was augmented by direct fire from below, coming through the burning roof. O'Malley and Robinson had by then received severe burns. Both had had their hair on fire and their eyebrows and lashes burned off. A bomb was rolled from the barracks towards Treacy's party. Seán picked it up and flung it back. The barracks burned and the complete garri-son withdrew to the lean-to.

The lively and daring action of the IRA destroyed the building but achieved little else. No arms were taken and the garrison held firm in the outhouse until daylight when the IRA called off the fight. Soon after, O'Malley, Seán Treacy, Séamus Robinson and the local battalion commandant were wrecking an army rifle range at Reehil when they were nearly surprised by a military patrol and their prisoners singing 'The Soldier's Song'. Treacy attacked them single-handed, managing to free all but two IRA prisoners they were holding. Separated from Treacy and not knowing what was happening, the others managed to escape in the darkness. Two days later, the newspapers told of a British patrol beating off two hundred armed men and capturing prisoners.

In June preparations were begun by Seán Treacy for an attack on Drangan barracks. He had succeeded in preparing a gelignite and clay mixture to stick to buildings and hoped for a surprise explosion. Fire was opened on IRA Volunteers approaching the barracks, however. Treacy dashed to the fray accompanied by Robinson and Tom O'Donovan. They adopted a procedure not unlike that at Hollyford, but this attack proved more fruitful. O'Malley took surrender of the garrison's weapons before Sergeant O'Sullivan marched out his constables with their hands held high. O'Malley was again badly burned — this time by a blazing beam as he dashed in to retrieve a box of ammunition. The barracks was destroyed.

Throughout the summer more British troops were being landed in Ireland. Sir Hamar Greenwood was telling the *Chicago Tribune,* 'We won't stand for independence, we won't have a republic. Short of that, if this campaign of violence and anarchy ceases, the Irish people can have any measure of Home Rule they can agree on!'

A man of method, Ernie O'Malley liked to have three sets of manuals, nominal rolls, regulations and other paperwork available for his organisational missions. One was retained at his headquarters in Dublin, another at his base in the area of operation. Upon his person, in his patched and torn clothing, strapped about his waist in specially reinforced moleskin pouches, he kept his 'field' set. Binoculars were slung about his neck and he kept his personal belongings in a haversack. 'I was my own base, and I looked it,' he said. Because of his strange appearance, he was fired on by the IRA on one occasion. They mistook him for a British officer.

His personal weapons during this period have often been disputed. Major Richard J. Keogh of Honolulu, writing in the American journal *Arms Gazette* on 'The Luger in Ireland' stated that when O'Malley operated in the open country he used a Model 1896 Mauser with a wooden holster-stock. He also carried a Winchester rifle, so he was extremely well armed. His urban armament was a Luger and a Smith and Wesson ·45 revolver. He had a narrow escape in a house where he was billeted when a girl accidentally discharged Ernie's own weapon and just missed him.

June saw an RIC mutiny at Listowel and a British army mutiny at Jullunder in India — both protesting against Black and Tan atrocities and oppressive measures. O'Malley and his Tipperary colleagues were back in action at Rear Cross Barracks on 11 July.

This time, O'Malley, Treacy and Gorman were the rooftop fire kindlers as men from north and south Tipperary and east Limerick, about fifty in all, fired on the barracks at the command of Paddy Dwyer. After nearly five hours of fighting, with the barracks in flames and its garrison being called upon to surrender, an RIC sergeant came to the door. He was silhouetted by the flames within but he bravely called that if the attack was not called off he would shoot the men on the roof. The three were sitting targets, but Paddy Dwyer shot down the sergeant before he could carry out his threat. Treacy, Gorman, Breen and O'Malley were wounded, Ernie by schrapnel in the shoulder. Rear Cross is often cited as the fiercest of all the barracks attacks. O'Malley collapsed after the fray.

London's *Weekly Dispatch* was claiming that 'the military scheme of enforcing law and order in Ireland will be perfected in a fortnight', even as O'Malley was presenting

GHQ with a brief on the formation of a Tipperary flying column as envisaged by Seán Treacy. Cardinal Logue was saying that 'the Holy Father is most anxious that Ireland should have her rights and full share of national prosperity, but also that Ireland should abstain from anything contrary to the law of God.'

The Pope was being pressed by the British foreign office to denounce all incitements to disturbance in Ireland and to personally make appointments to vacant Irish bishoprics. They did not trust the choices of the diocesan clergy. The Vatican replied in the negative.

By that time Ernie O'Malley was discussing incitement in Cork with Liam Lynch, who had captured Brigadier General Lucas of the Shropshire Regiment as he was fishing on the Blackwater. He was also advising on the formation of a north Cork flying column, even as Terence MacSwiney was beginning his hunger strike.

Good intelligence work, thorough preparation which took cognisance of all contingencies, sensible scouting and level-headed determination were all in evidence during O'Malley's engagement with the Second Cork Brigade at Mallow on the night of 27-28 September 1920. He was supporting Liam Lynch in what has been claimed as the only capture of a military barracks in Ireland by the IRA.

The post was occupied by the 17th Lancers, whose crest was a death's head and who were dubbed 'The Death or Glories'. The newly-formed flying column of Lynch's brigade brought off the coup. Acting as scouts in a complicated manoeuvre were the local Mallow company who steered the raiders through the constant patrols of military and Black and Tans.

Two of the barrack maintenance staff, Jack Bolster and Dick Willis, reported on the movements of guards, sentries and look-outs within the gates. They provided sketches and answered questions put to them by Lynch, Paddy O'Brien, George Power and Ernie O'Malley. Willis brought Lynch and O'Malley on a tour of the barrack surrounds and the area where the Lancer officers exercised their horses each morning.

On the morning of the raid the local RIC barracks was covered by Volunteers. Paddy McCarthy of Newmarket posing as a Board of Works overseer, entered with Willis and Bolster.

When the officers cantered out on their horses they left an NCO, Sergeant Gibbs, in charge of the post. Ernie O'Malley approached the gate and presented a bogus letter for personal delivery to a member of the garrison. He was refused admission but he overpowered the gatekeeper sentry and waved on the remainder of the attacking party to take over the guardroom. Gibbs rushed to train a machine-gun on the now wide open main gate. One burst of fire would have wiped out the attackers so he was shot, and he fell. After IRA Volunteers had cut all communications into Mallow, motor cars were driven into the barracks and loaded with captured weapons and ammuniton even as the last of the garrison were being disarmed and held. Field dressings were applied to Gibbs' wound but he was past medical help. Up to thirty assorted arms and some bayonets were captured.

Members of the column spread straw and petrol with the intention of firing the barracks but the urgent shrill blast of the retreat whistle signal prevented this operation being completed. Men jumped into cars, well satisfied with their success. As they passed along the road, willing hands sawed down trees in their wake. Mesmerised officers dismounted their chargers. Awe changed to anger and an enraged garrison began a campaign of arson and general destruction of property in the town and its hinterland.

The arms captured at Mallow were used a month later when the column, under O'Malley and Lynch and supported by Newmarket and Kanturk battalions under Seán Moylan, Denis Galvin, Dan Vaughan and Seán Nunan ambushed a convoy at Ballydrahane. There was one British casualty and more arms were captured.

It was about this time that Seán Moylan made his celebrated attempt to put an old cannon taken from Ross Castle in Killarney to functional use. Ernie O'Malley was an enthusiastic assistant in the abortive experiment. This was a little light relief among tragic events for Ernie and his colleagues. Dan Breen was injured in Dublin, Seán Treacy was shot dead in Talbot Street, Terence MacSwiney died after his long hunger strike. Brigadier General Cockriel made an unheeded appeal through *The Times* for an unconditional truce. On 1 November, Kevin Barry was executed.

As the year 1920 petered out, some of the most significant events of the War of Independence were taking place. In the early hours of 4 November twenty men of the North Longford Column under the command of Seán Mac Eoin successfully defended the village of Ballinalee from about a hundred rampaging Black and Tans. In Dublin on the morning of 21 November members of Michael Collins' Intelligence Section executed fourteen British agents; that afternoon in retaliation, Crown forces fired into a football match at Croke Park killing twelve players and spectators. O'Malley was in Dublin on this day which became known as Bloody Sunday, but was not involved. After midnight, Dick McKee, Peadar Clancy and Conor Clune were shot dead in Dublin Castle, allegedly while trying to escape. On 28 November Tom Barry and the West Cork Flying Column ambushed a convoy of the hated Auxiliaries at Kilmichael killing sixteen. Fr O'Flanagan made his controversial move of sending a telegram to Lloyd George aimed at bringing about peace proposals. The Auxiliaries and Black and Tans burned Cork city on 11 December and Canon Magner was shot dead on 15 December; his murderer was judged insane. On 18 December Bishop Cohalan issued an excommunication decree against the IRA. It was said that Dan Breen and Seán O'Hegarty were planning an episcopal hanging in reprisal! On Christmas Eve, de Valera arrived back from the United States.

Ernie O'Malley was not enjoying his Christmas. In the early part of December, using the alias of 'Bernard Stewart', he travelled to Co Kilkenny to prepare for an attack on the Auxiliaries at Inistiogue. Kilkenny veterans of the War of Independence took exception to O'Malley's later utterances about the state of readiness within the county. They also resented his remarks about the local commandant Jim O'Hanrahan suggesting some incompetence in the leader, who was well respected.

It was O'Hanrahan who brought Ernie on a tour of the lovely Kilkenny riverland and who gave him hospitality, food and rest. The house was raided and both Ernie and O'Hanrahan were taken into custody, along with a young boy on the run named Holland. Holland and 'Stewart' were tied up, interrogated and beaten, and when they did not respond, cast into a cold, wet cellar. The Auxiliaries used their old ploy of pretending to prepare for the men's execution.

If Ernie spoke ill of O'Hanrahan, the detraction was reciprocated with reference to this arrest. O'Hanrahan claimed afterwards that O'Malley foolishly carried about nominal rolls of IRA Volunteers in his area, that these were captured on his arrest and that the men were harassed thereafter.

O'Malley pulled faces when his captors attempted to take a photograph. This brought a threat of being bayoneted. While being moved to Dublin he was taken aback at the nonchalance of the convoy commander when a civilian was knocked down and killed *en route*. (There is some evidence to suggest that Ernie's brother Frank was approached in Nigeria in an effort to get information on his whereabouts. Those who questioned Frank did not know that the hunted man was in their custody as 'Bernard Stewart'.) He was lodged in the guardroom of the Castle initially but was later placed in a cell with the Capuchin Fr Dominick who was sympathetic towards Volunteers. Then followed more interrogations, more threatened executions — even to the point of firing blank rounds. The notorious Captain Hardy was his tormentor.

In the New Year, O'Malley was moved to Kilmainham. He found it damp, smelly, cold and poorly lit. Fr Dominick was court-martialled and imprisoned for possessing an incriminating document. A newspaper slipped under O'Malley's door reported a raid on Eileen McGrane's flat. There they found notebooks belonging to him but his illegible handwriting posed difficulties for them. Fortunately they did not associate their captive, who was still masquerading as a farmer from Kilkenny, with the perpetrator of the documents.

Many of the prisoners, including O'Malley, were suspected of having taken part in the Bloody Sunday operation. One of these was young Paddy Moran of Crossna, Co Roscommon, who was tried and sentenced to death. He was so sure of his innocence that he firmly believed he would not be executed and so he refused an offer to join in an escape bid with O'Malley; he was hanged on 14 March 1921. Frank Teeling, wounded and captured at Mount Street on 'Bloody Sunday' and sentenced to death, befriended a sentry. Volunteer contacts on the outside coordinated a plan with this man to allow the escape of Teeling, O'Malley and Simon Donnelly. Some commentators say that the sentry acutally joined the IRA. They condemn the fact that he was afterwards forgotten about as he served a life sentence at Dartmoor for his action.

The plan envisaged the escapees reaching a wall where a rope would be thrown over to allow them to climb it. Courting couples outside upset things and they had to be 'kidnapped'. But the rope broke and the attempt had to be made another night.

This time a bolt cutter was supplied to shear the catch on the small gate. Paddy Moran organised a concert within the prison as a distraction, and O'Malley, Teeling and Donnelly walked out to freedom.

Ernie's alias was now 'O'Brien'. He lay low in Dublin until called one day to meet Collins, de Valera and Mulcahy. He thought the meeting might be to discuss a proposed military college in Dublin. After a three-hour discussion, he was given command of the Second Southern Division with brigades in Limerick, Kilkenny and Tipperary — five in all.

His arrival was awaited with interest. He began a tour of inspection. When he came to Limerick great pains were taken to procure fine quarters for the divisional commander. He had a name for being fastidious about food so the best victuals were laid on for him. He remarked:'If you thought less of your bellies and more about what you're supposed to be doing, you'd be better off.'

On 24 April 1921 Ernie presided at a meeting in Kippagh, Co Cork. He did not greatly impress the Corkmen with his talk laden with military terminology. (Tom Barry especially took a dislike to him.) They felt that the setting up of a division on paper was meaningless under local circumstances. However, the First Southern Division was formed and Liam Lynch was given command. Ernie returned thereafter to his own Second Southern Division.

Peace moves were beginning and Lord Derby visited Dublin, but the execution of four IRA members who had been captured after the Dripsey ambush in Cork did not help to calm affairs in the south. There was considerable action against Crown forces in the First Division area but O'Malley's division appeared to be quietly preparing rather than rushing into any precipitate action.

On 25 May Dublin's Custom House was burned. Ernie's brother Cecil was arrested. He too was a medical student. A colleague of his was shot dead when the two young men tried to escape and a false rumour spread that Cecil had been killed. The O'Malley family tragedy worsened when Frank died in Dar-es-Salaam on 19 June.

Ernie and Liam Lynch worked closely in planning for the future. O'Malley carried out strict inspections and attended to the unpleasant duty of executing three British officers. Activities were winding down, however, and at noon on 11 July a Truce agreement between Britain and Ireland came into operation. General Dick Mulcahy signed the order suspending further operations.

# 3

# Truce, Treaty and Civil War

*To the walls flew Grace O'Malley*
*With her clansmen at her side*
*Who had often met the foemen*
*On the land and on the tide.*
*But she saw the marshalled strength*
*Of the English coming on*
*And the colour of their armour*
*That in polished brightness shone.*

The Truce followed an intensive period of negotiation in which the South African premier General Smuts and other prominent people played a part. Formal talks on a more permanent peace began in London in October. The Irish delegation consisted of Arthur Griffith, Michael Collins, Robert Barton, George Gavan Duffy, Eamon Duggan and Erskine Childers (with three assistants) as secretary.

O'Malley was not convinced of the wisdom of the Truce and was abrupt at GHQ meetings. He was also highly critical of the much-lauded Thompson gun, then being introduced. This weapon which was to become a rallying symbol within the IRA had earlier been demonstrated to the RIC in Dublin by the explorer Mitchel Hedges, but the British government lost interest. Around the same time a consignment of five hundred was seized by New York customs' officials. The shipment had been arranged by Laurence de Lacy in the wake of the smuggling in of the first two Thompsons for Sinn Féin by James Dineen and Patrick Cronin. Another shipment got through, however.

In the early days of the Truce, O'Malley learned to drive — though not too well, as terrified passengers later testified. He struck a monument in Mullingar on one occasion and severely damaged the car he was driving. One night he ran out of fuel but managed to buy a can of petrol from the RIC driver of a Crossley tender.

There was considerable traffic to and from London about this time. Strangely, the Truce did not debar purchase of arms, and war souvenirs were freely available in England. A sympathetic member of the British Boys' Brigade in Rugby forwarded his personal carbine to Desmond Fitzgerald's brother Frank in London — simply by putting a label on it with Fitzgerald's address. O'Malley and Johnny Raleigh travelled over. Tom Barry followed a little later. O'Malley was concerned at Barry's expense sheet and commented that Raleigh and himself stayed longer, bought more 'stuff', yet had less expenses. He instructed that no officer was entitled to spend money on clothes without direct sanction from himself and added that such an unnecessary expense would have to stop immediately. (Barry had purchased arms to the value of £14.10s.6d and clothes costing £13.8s.3d.)

Ernie called on Collins and Diarmuid O'Hegarty, one of Childers' assistants, in Cadogan Gardens on a few occasions. He later alluded to a certain amount of lavish living by members of the deputation. Kathleen Napoli McKenna, secretary to Desmond Fitzgerald and Erskine Childers in the department of publicity, later denied emphatically that such was the case and added that Miss O'Donoghue (brought over from the Gresham) provided good meals. Erskine Childers organised one party for the overworked staff. However, she repudiated any suggestion of overspending.

The Treaty was signed in London in the early hours of 6 December 1921 and the Dáil began debating the issue on 14 December. Many IRA men agreed with the view expressed by Ernie's old comrade Deputy Séamus Robinson, O/C South Tipperary Brigade, during the debate; he felt that the army should have been consulted about the Treaty. He pointed out that, despite the Oath of Allegiance to Dáil Éireann, the army was under the control of the Army Executive.

There was little difference of opinion between Barry and

O'Malley concerning the Treaty. They both opposed it vehemently and had been troubled by de Valera's reputation as a moderate until Dev personally declared to them that privately he advocated confronting British troops each month.

However, on 7 January 1922 the Dáil approved the Treaty by sixty-four votes to fifty-seven. On the 9th, Arthur Griffith was elected president in place of de Valera and Dick Mulcahy became minister for defence in place of Cathal Brugha. A pencilled note of Frank Aiken, written on 10 January, recalls Griffith stating that he would keep the Republic in being until the establishment of the Free State and Mulcahy's assurance: 'The army will remain the army of the Republic.'* Aiken recorded that late in the evening nearly all officers of GHQ staff and officers commanding divisions and independent brigades met in the Mansion House. Lynch nearly broke down as he vowed to take no more orders from GHQ. Frank Aiken adequately conveyed the turmoil of mind which possessed many of those involved. He found himself against the Treaty but having reliance in the promises being made. He appreciated the difficulties in which the plenipotentiaries found themselves and admitted to a possibility that he would have voted for the Treaty if he had been a member. Notable absentees from the meeting were Cathal Brugha, Liam Mellows, Rory O'Connor and Ernie O'Malley.

On the following day, 11 January, a letter requesting a General Army Convention was delivered to Mulcahy. Rory O'Connor led the signatories; O'Malley did not sign. His was the most blatant opposition to the army coming under the control of the Provisional Government. Even when he was appointed, along with Oscar Traynor, to attend army council meetings for the purpose of keeping a watching brief, he declined. Instead, he went back to his division and announced that he would not recognise the minister for defence nor his chief-of-staff; in fact he would refuse to obey any orders from them.

Collins was severely worried about O'Malley's action,

* O'Malley Papers, University College Dublin Archives, p. 17B/93.

just as he was about that of Tom Hales, Liam Deasy and others. He was convinced that if he could personally explain the situation to them, they would recognise the Treaty as the 'stepping stone' envisaged by him, but the Provisional Government was establishing its headquarters in City Hall. A regular army had to be established from the Volunteers. Attention to the recognised danger had to be deferred.

The withdrawing British were recalling weapons for storage in various RIC barracks. O'Malley led a raid on Clonmel in February and seized arms and ammunition. He had again availed of inside information to obtain the password which one member of the raiding party used to gain admission. He then held up the guard until the raiders rushed in and loaded the booty into assorted vehicles, whereupon the whole party dashed away, well satisfied with their seizure. This action was in direct violation of the Treaty at a time when its most vehement opponents were still acting within the terms laid down by the Dáil. It was almost as if O'Malley was repudiating suggestions that he had at one stage supported the Treaty. Details of this very significant event were not recorded in *The Singing Flame*.

In Limerick Liam Forde issued a proclamation repudiating GHQ authority to take over barracks in his brigade area from the British. Michael Brennan, pro-Treaty, was ordered over from Clare to take over posts in the city. Boundaries had not hitherto been crossed in this way. There was anger among anti-Treaty sections of Limerick's community. John Hurley, local pro-Treaty captain, acted wisely and tried to organise a take-over by Limerick men, but he was arrested by anti-Treatyites who were now descending on the city from all parts. O'Malley arrived from Tipperary to take over Castle Barracks, the old fortress on the town's defences dating from 1200 and called after King John. Plans went awry and he and his party were forced to spend the night in the mental hospital. Next day he occupied the Glentworth and Royal George hotels. There he met with GHQ officers and both sides exchanged ultimatums to vacate the city. A tense situation existed.

Eventually Liam Lynch was called in and, with Oscar Traynor, a settlement formula was worked out which had the approval of the chief-of-staff. Limerick corporation were to take over four police barracks and a small maintenance party — responsible to Lynch — was to be installed in each of the two military barracks. Liam Lynch later expressed pleasure at the important peace-keeping role played by him. He saw up to 700 men, earlier primed for a fight, leave Limerick city. Massive bloodshed had been averted. Of this event, Michael McInerney wrote in the *Irish Times:* 'He even risked launching his own private Civil War in Limerick . . . when Collins and Mulcahy had to restrain Griffith from attacking him.'

Postponements of the Army Convention resulted in the anti-Treaty officers holding their own sessions on 26 March and 9 April. No Treaty supporters were in attendance. The stated objects of the anti-Treaty officers were aired. These included the maintenance of the Irish Republic's independence and the protection of the liberties and rights of the Irish people. It pledged service to an established republican government upholding such objects. It elected an executive of sixteen members, including Ernie O'Malley. He and Seán MacBride carried out the secretarial duties associated with the convention.

This body issued an instruction that all anti-Treaty members of the IRA should report to their units, even as it announced that it refused to recognise further the authority of the minister for defence or the chief-of-staff of the national army. It called on the Provisional Government to cease recruiting for this army and for the Civic Guards.

From the executive was drawn the army council, in which O'Malley figured as director of organisation. Liam Lynch was chief-of-staff with Joe McKelvey his deputy. Florence O'Donoghue was adjutant general and Liam Mellows was quartermaster general.

Recognising the serious situation developing, efforts were made by moderates on both sides to effect a reconciliation. By now, however, some barracks and posts taken over from the British were in the hands of Treaty sup-

porters while others were garrisoned by anti-Treaty troops.
On 13 April, the Four Courts, Inns Quay, Dublin, was
occupied by anti-Treaty forces who established a headquarters there.

Deliberations continued between former comrades in
arms whose minds were troubled, whose hearts were
heavy. On the question of armed resistance in the six north-
eastern counties both forces found common ground. Dick
Mulcahy was working towards placing Frank Aiken in
charge of all northern sections of the army in order to pur-
sue this policy. A pact was signed between de Valera and
Collins and another effort to re-unite the army began.
Ernie O'Malley was appointed, along with Liam Lynch,
Seán Moylan, and Rory O'Connor, to represent the anti-
Treaty side at a conference with Dick Mulcahy, Gearóid
O'Sullivan, Seán McMahon and Eoin O'Duffy.

The meeting failed to agree on appointments and caused
some disunity among the Four Courts garrison. O'Malley
felt that Lynch was conceding too much and indeed when
the deputation reported back to the Four Courts his stand
was supported. The proposed appointment of a pro-Treaty
minister for defence and chief-of-staff was resented, particularly when their deputies were to be taken from the anti-
Treaty side. It was decided to discontinue negotiations.
Liam Lynch was disappointed and is quoted as having
remarked, 'I'm going south. I'm not thinking of war, I'm
thinking of peace.'

Ernie O'Malley and Rory O'Connor were authorised to
proceed to the national army headquarters at Beggarsbush
and present General Mulcahy with a copy of the resolu-
tions passed. These stipulated that army reunification
negotiations should cease, that no offensive would be taken
against the 'Beggarsbush troops' but that necessary action
would be taken to 'maintain the Republic against British
aggression'. Envisaged by the final statement was a plan to
attack British troops still resident in their Phoenix Park
headquarters.

Meanwhile, O'Malley was continuing with daring enter-
prises. He brought an armoured car from Tipperary and

collected some weapons along the way back to the Four
Courts. He was involved in collecting arms from sympathisers in the Curragh and from the new Civic Guard barracks
in Kildare town. He locked Liam Lynch and Cathal Brugha
out of the Four Courts as well as others who opposed the
idea of war against the British.

Sir Henry Wilson, chief of imperial general staff and
close associate of Lloyd George, was shot dead in London
on 22 June. The incident sparked a paranoiac condemna-
tion of the Four Courts occupation which was climaxed on
26 June when Winston Churchill said:

> If it doesn't come to an end, if through weakness, want
> of courage, or some other even less creditable reason it
> is not brought to an end, and a speedy end, then it is my
> duty to say, on behalf of His Majesty's Government,
> that we shall regard the Treaty as having been formally
> violated.

Lloyd George stated that the British government's views
had been conveyed to the Provisional Government and
added, 'I would rather they acted upon their own initiative,
rather than with the appearance that they are doing it
under compulsion from the British government.'

An assault on the north was still being prepared — the
Four Courts garrison organising it to the knowledge of both
sides. While arranging transport for the movement of arms,
Leo Henderson was arrested. This came as a surprise to the
garrison, but they reacted quickly by deciding on a retali-
atory apprehension. Seán MacBride had been recently promoted from staff captain to staff commandant and assistant
director of organisation to Ernie O'Malley at the anti-
Treaty headquarters. These two men were having morning
coffee with Maureen Buckley and Eileen McGilligan in
Bewley's on the morning after the Henderson arrest when
O'Malley said, 'Come on and we'll capture O'Connell.'
They went to the private home of McGilligan's in Leeson
Street and informed J. J. (Ginger) O'Connell, deputy
chief-of-staff of the national army, that they were arresting
him. The slightly bemused lieutenant general was taken
quietly to the Four Courts and held captive. He was not the

only prisoner there. Seán MacBride had been bearer of despatches between Dublin and London during the Treaty negotiations, and long before that he had been working closely with Collins and Tobin in the business of procuring armaments. He dealt with ex-First World War officers in Germany through an American middle-man named Hoover, said to have been related to Herbert Clark Hoover, later President of the USA. Vendors felt that Hoover was making an unrealistic profit on the deal and told MacBride there would be no further negotiations until he was out of the way. Seán brought him back to Dublin and locked him up in the Four Courts. This explains rumours which circulated about the part being played in the drama by an 'important, loudly dressed American'. MacBride was still in close contact with Collins because of the proposed raid on the north, so he did not reveal Hoover's true identity. Even within the building there were doubts. Some did not like Seán and Ernie frequenting Bewleys, for Ernest Bewley was deemed to be a West Briton — although in a 'lighter kind of way', it was conceded.

With the capture of O'Connell, however, along with other considerations, a showdown with the Four Courts garrison by national troops was inevitable. The building itself, designed by Gandon, was a magnificent example of eighteenth century classicism. On 28 June 1922 Ordnance QF 18 Pounder Mark II No. 10756 was aimed — or more correctly, pointed — at the Four Courts by Johnny Doyle, a captain in the national army. Many rounds were wide of their mark, which brought protests from various sources. From Wednesday to Friday the shelling continued from a position south of the river near Winetavern Street.

Liam Mellows and Rory O'Connor were in the Four Courts, Liam Lynch, still in contact with Mellows, was downriver in the Clarence Hotel and Oscar Traynor commanded the Dublin Brigade from an O'Connell Street hotel. Cumann na mBan women liaised between groups. Paddy O'Brien was in command at the Four Courts. Seán Lemass was adjutant and Seán Nolan was quartermaster.

He controlled some of the arms still coming from Beggars-bush right up to the evening before the shelling. A party set off to Donegal with them that night.

The Four Courts garrison never stood a chance. They used their armoured car and machine guns to good effect, but they had little food and no sleep throughout the shelling, which lasted three days. The gun history-sheet of the 18 pounder showed that a total of 375 rounds were fired during the operation. Paddy O'Brien was injured. Evacuation of the garrison was discussed but was deemed unrealistic. Fr Albert, acting as chaplain, urged surrender.

In his book, *The Singing Flame*, Ernie O'Malley described the trauma of surrendering having taken over command from Paddy O'Brien, while eight hundred years of historical documentation blazed and the magnificent building was crumbling in a blasted, burned-out pyre.

According to some sources, including Ernie, Paddy Daly and Tony Lawlor accepted the surrender. Peadar O'Donnell thought it was a friend of his, Paddy O'Connor. He said to O'Connor, 'Oh, Paddy, you're in charge. I'm going off so!' O'Connor said, 'Good luck to you.' But Peadar checked with Rory O'Connor who felt that the members of the executive should stick together and take whatever was going.

Peadar, Ernie and others were then taken prisoner and brought to Jameson's Distillery at Bow Street. As they were escorted away by national troops an old woman made the wry observation: 'Thanks be to jaysus they're in the hands of their own.'

Paddy O'Connor was in Bow Street too and he arranged that a friendly sentry would be placed in charge of them. This provided Ernie O'Malley, Seán Lemass and four others with a chance to escape. Asked why he did not make a run for it himself, Peadar O'Donnell said, 'I was too busy getting the rest of them away.'

Peadar O'Donnell was critical of the lack of coherence within the IRA executive around that time. 'They had no policy at all,' he said. He pointed out that men like Pilkington, Kilroy and others had taken an oath to the Republic and had fought on its behalf but they were incapable of coming down to earth. 'They made martyrs, not revolutionaries,' he said. He thought Ernie O'Malley would have been a better selection for chief-of-staff than Lynch, whose appointment came about mainly on the strength of his command in the First Southern Division, which carried a certain degree of seniority.

'Although Ernie was not a man of strong social ideals,' said Peadar, '. . . he would come down on the right side. . .' While some commanders did not feel at home with him, they had admiration for his record of courage and daring in the War of Independence. Furthermore, Peadar thought Ernie was 'discerning of make-believe activists'. Yet he was also patient with people who pretended to be more than they were. O'Donnell regarded Ernie as 'one of the great figures of the republican movement, superior in stature to Mulcahy, Mac Eoin and many others.'

Fighting continued in other parts of Dublin. Cecil Malley, Ernie's brother was twenty years old and in command of the Gresham Hotel garrison. Another brother, eighteen-year-old Charlie, was killed in the fighting off the lane behind that hotel. Ernie O'Malley wished to meet forces which were moving from Tipperary to assist the Dublin garrison. W. J. Brennan-Whitmore drove to Dublin and parked his car at Woods of Donnybrook. It so happened that this was the car which Ernie seized to make his getaway. He knew the house because Tony Woods had been in the Four Courts with him, but he did not know the car belonged to a guest. He made contact with the troops at Blessington, but Oscar Traynor had ordered the force not to move into the city. Peadar O'Donnell later expressed surprise that O'Malley, as director of operations, did not override Traynor's order. Perhaps Ernie's decision was based on his study of military chain of command which would not condone such action by a staff officer within the area of responsibility of a field commander.

Some of the party remained to fight in Baltinglass but Ernie left to organise the occupation of Enniscorthy as a citadel for the formation of a south-eastern command.

Lynch moved to Clonmel from where he hoped to organise a line of resistance across the country. 'A ridiculous idea,' said Peadar O'Donnell. 'The Free Staters simply went by sea and landed at Cork.' This was a reference to the voyage of the *Lady Wicklow* and the *Arvonia* which took place at a later date.

Meanwhile Ernie O'Malley, Joe Griffin and others were operating in the Wicklow-Wexford area and attempting to establish part of this line in the Carlow-Kilkenny area. They were not very successful and Ernie was soon back in a Dublin headquarters with Madge Clifford as secretary. He attempted to organise a small operational column among headquarters staff, but arrests and general harassment prevented any progress. Todd Andrews assisted him, and young Kevin Malley, then only fifteen years of age, was a dedicated courier although he suffered from infantile paralysis. Ernie worked on a plan of isolating Dublin by destroying bridges, railway lines, roads and telephone exchanges. Men were moved into position early in August but many of them were captured and nothing came of the effort. Arthur Griffith died and then Michael Collins was shot dead in an ambush. Ernie felt that this was a very bad day for Ireland.

Ernie moved his office to the house of a priest for a while. He also returned home to Glasnevin in September for the first time since May 1918. Many things had happened. Frank was dead and buried in East Africa; Albert, called 'Bertie' was abroad in the Nigerian Frontier Force; Charlie was dead and Cecil had just been imprisoned. He went to visit his sister Kathleen at Miss Gavan Duffy's Scoil Bríde on St Stephen's Green. She had been warned that if any visitor said he was Ernie to look for the scar on his upper lip. He satisfied her that he was indeed her brother — all the more when he brought her to the Cafe Cairo and treated her to tea and buns. She remembered him telling her the waitresses there looked after all the men 'on the run' when they were hungry.

Ernie received a note written by Rory O'Connor in Mountjoy on 12 September. It told him of a tunnel leading to the Four Courts which could be used if they had left any important documents behind. One piece of folklore attached to that area of the city concerned a tunnel from there to Christchurch, built in the thirteenth century when a Dominican friary of St Saviour occupied the Four Courts site. Towards the end of the nineteenth century, an army officer was accidentally locked in the tunnel which was used for storing ceremonial paraphernalia. He was soon documented as 'missing, presumed dead' until the next occasion demanding the opening of the tunnel. Near its entrance was discovered the skeleton of the officer and in the bones of his right hand was his sword. Lying about were the broken bone-fragments of up to 250 rats that had attacked and had been beaten off by the man's sword before he himself was overcome.

Perhaps Ernie O'Malley knew the story. Perhaps he even contemplated using the tunnel for he and his staff were now being closely watched, and observed by the press too. As acting assistant chief-of-staff he wrote a letter of warning to J. E. Healy, editor of the *Irish Times:*

To: Mr J. E. Healy        Field Headquarters
Irish Times       Northern & Eastern Command
                             21st September 1922


A warning recently addressed to certain newspapers in Dublin has been ignored.

[No change in tone of Journals since warning delivered.] Staff of Command has decided that by allowing the present paper campaign to continue they would be committing a crime against the REPUBLIC.

The following alternatives are open to you:

1. Conduct your paper as a genuine Free Press or
2. Hand over your Journal to the Free State Authorities to be conducted officially by them.

Failure to comply to be regarded as determination to use the Press as a military weapon against the REPUBLIC and will involve the same risks for you as are run by armed soldiers of the Free State Provisional Government.

Todd Andrews was inspecting northern units about this time and his reports to Ernie were outspoken. A typical letter: 'O/C Brigade arrived two hours late and having talked at length about patriotism etc. VETOED the column idea.'

Then there came the bishops' joint pastoral of 10 October which was issued by the hierarchy to the priests and people of Ireland. All resistance to the Provisional Government was condemned and acts of aggression leading to the death of national troops were regarded as murder. Divisional commander of the (anti-Treaty) Northern Divison Seán Lehane wrote to O'Malley:

> What does GHQ decide on for dealing with the priests etc. I had a note from C. Daly who is in west Donegal during the past fortnight, in which he states that the confessionals are used for getting information. Youngsters are scared into giving information to the clergy. In east Donegal (where we are at present) the Protestants are by far our best friends, the reason being I suppose, that they are free from Church tyranny.

The report was fairly typical of the reaction. A religious man, Ernie O'Malley was not unduly worried. He went to the wooden chapel in Glasnevin each Saturday where Fr Dudley, his regular confessor, found no difficulty in giving him absolution.

Todd Andrews wrote in his book *Dublin Made Me:*

> To us who were in arms against the acceptance of the Treaty it appeared not merely intemperate in its language but vindictive in its spirit. . . They said that we had deliberately set out to make our motherland a heap of ruins. By insensate blockades, we were seeking to starve the people or bring them into social stagnation. The war we were waging was a system of plunder and assassination. Our young lives, they said, were utterly spoiled by early association with cruelty and robbery, falsehood and crime. They were unable to understand how, within a few months, we had changed from being generous, kind-hearted and good and became involved in a network of crime.

Peadar O'Donnell wryly stated that we were never a priest-ridden country, but that we had a yahoo-ridden priesthood.

Stronger warnings were issued to the press and the *Daily Bulletin* called on de Valera to make representations to the Vatican 'formally and emphatically' protesting against the 'unwarrantable action of the Irish hierarchy in presuming and pretending to pronounce an authoritative judgement upon the question of constitutional and political fact now at issue in Ireland.'

O'Malley passed around a book called *The Ruin of Education in Ireland* by F. Hugh O'Donnell. This recalled the Greek Orthodox Church's organisation, Fanar, which kept Greek subjects quiescent at the behest of the Turks. It suggested that the Irish Church was behaving similarly. Ernie resented the Church 'placing God on the side of the Treaty!'

Special powers and martial law granted by the Dáil to the national army took effect and the anti-Treaty executive met in Ballybacon near the beautiful Glen of Aherlow. Ernie O'Malley joined Lynch, Deasy, Robinson, Moylan, Derrig, Barrett, O'Connor, Whelan and Barry. They resolved to call for a government which would preserve the continuity of a republic. They empowered it to 'make an arrangement with the Free State government' — even with the British government, as long as the country was not brought into the empire. De Valera was to be president.

# 4

## Capture

*On the walls of Carrick Clooney*
*As the summer sun went down*
*And its last bright rays were fading*
*On the spires of Newport town.*
*To the watchmen on the ramparts*
*There appeared in long array*
*A band of raiding spearmen*
*By the waters of Clew Bay.*

Ernie O'Malley moved his office to 36 Ailesbury Road where the Humphreys family lived. Mrs Humphreys was the widow of Dr David Humphreys of Limerick. Her sister Áine kept her company. Their brother The O'Rahilly was killed during Easter Week 1916.

Mrs Humphreys' children Sighle, Emmet and Dick had been influenced by their aunt Áine during stays in Parteen, Co. Clare so that now they were deeply involved in anti-Treaty activities. Sighle was in Cumann na mBan and had been ferrying guns around Donegal on the eve of the Four Courts shelling. Dick had been imprisoned and had undergone a hunger strike in 1919. As a member of Fianna Éireann he had gone to the GPO in 1916, where Padraic Pearse had told him to go home. The lad was crestfallen, but Pearse consoled him by saying that if anything happened to his uncle there would be no man of the house at 40 Herbert Park, where the family then lived. Emmet Humphreys was in prison at this time.

The Herbert Park house was still occupied by Madame O'Rahilly in the autumn of 1922. Mary MacSwiney, sister of Terence, stayed there too.

Madge Clifford called daily to the Humphreys and carried out secretarial duties for Ernie O'Malley. Sighle

looked after his personal needs. It was often said that
Sighle was 'doing a line' with Ernie. This type of rumour
was inevitable because the Cumann na mBan girls, out of a
sense of duty, paid attention to the men on the run. Sighle
admitted to having been fond of Ernie. 'But then I was fond
of them all, especially Liam Mellows,' she said, and she
insisted that Frank Aiken was far more popular with the
girls. 'Despatches for the Fourth Northern were in great
demand.' The women worshipped Mick Price because he
trusted them implicitly, whereas they had to assert themselves to obtain due recognition from other leaders of the
time. 'But Ernie and I were really only sparring,' laughed
Sighle. Máire Comerford often acted as Ernie's despatch
courier and driver. On one occasion he nearly shot her in
error. Eileen McGrane was also a close associate.

Many writers have described O'Malley's hideout at the
Humphreys' home as a 'secret room'. It was no such thing.
Sighle logically explained the misnomer, for both the house
and the room were built by Batt O'Connor, staunch companion and confidant to Michael Collins. The existence of
the room would be well known, and indeed Mrs Humphreys pointed this out to Ernie when he occupied it.
O'Malley overlooked this in *The Singing Flame* when he
wrote: 'She thought the Staters did not know of the room
and her mind was at ease about it.'

However, Sighle was certain that when Batt O'Connor
'went the other way' after the Treaty he would have kept
quiet about the room. 'I don't believe he ever told about it.
When I meet him in Heaven, I'll ask him and I'll be very
disappointed if he says he did.'

A secret room was envisaged when the house was built
during the War of Independence, but its construction was
too closely scrutinised by Castle detectives. When the
building was completed, however, Batt O'Connor concealed a small sewing room at the end of a passage by
placing a large press across its entrance and employing a
system of wires and pulleys to gain admission. Cathal
Brugha had used the room during the War of Independence.

Ernie moved about on business fairly regularly, but Sighle denies reports of his being given to acts of bravado. Nevertheless he was in bad form one morning when his assistant Todd Andrews called. Grumpily he handed Andrews a ·45 Webley and pocketed one himself before enticing Todd to take a bus with him to Westland Row — for a haircut! Todd admitted, 'I was appalled. . . that the assistant chief-of-staff should be ready to expose himself to such unnecessary risks. I should of course have refused to go but I simply hadn't the moral courage to do so lest I should be thought "windy", which I was. To be "windy" was to be written off.'

Andrews became more concerned when they had to wait their turn. He was not at all amused when Ernie ordered a shave and shampoo as well as a haircut. He was downright convulsed when, after the treatment, O'Malley bought two large Corona cigars and lit up while awaiting their tram back.

We were simply not dressed for the part especially as Ernie wore a conspicuously large off-white woollen cap. I got off the tram at Appian Way getting rid of my half-smoked cigar as quickly as possible and made for the comfortable refuge of one of our safe houses nearby. As I sat over a cup of tea and emerged at last from my state of shock, I could only laugh at the sheer absurdity of the whole adventure; the picture of O'Malley and myself had something of the quality of a comic strip — Mutt and Jeff! I began too to reflect on the personality of Ernie O'Malley as exemplified by the impulsive folly which allowed him to risk his life (and worse still, mine) for a haircut. He was clearly unhappy being bound to a desk dispensing circulars to what at that time were mainly non-existent units of the IRA or, where they existed, rarely sent a reply. He would have achieved true fulfilment in leading a flying column or commando unit in the field and would have been a superb field commander.

Mrs Humphreys and Áine O'Rahilly arose early on the morning of 4 November. The servant girl Nellie began her daily chores while the pair went to Mass. The remainder of the household were still sleeping.

Army trucks trundled into the fashionable Ailesbury Road. Excited national soldiers alighted and crept along neatly tended gardens. They had orders to raid number 36 and, like all army orders, they were embellished by rumour. The rumour grew until many of the raiding party were convinced that they were about to effect the capture of Eamon de Valera. One of the raiding party was Bill McKenna, whose sister Kathleen had been secretary to Desmond Fitzgerald and Erskine Childers in the War of Independence days. He confirmed that many of the rank and file were of this opinion.

De Valera was in the district — over around Sandymount, it was thought — but it was to Ernie O'Malley's room that Sighle Humphreys ran to shout a warning when she was awakened by the sound of heavy and hurried footsteps on the gravel and the purr of slowing lorries.

Neighbours saw the troops surround the house and one of them ran to tell Mrs Humphreys and her sister at the church. They returned home immediately.

According to some reports, the national troops were fired on and pinned down as they approached the house. They took cover and had to await the arrival of reinforcements before rushing the building. They then burst in and made for the concealed room, splintering the woodwork of the press with revolver fire and battering it in with riflebutts. When an opening was hacked away, however, O'Malley rushed out, firing at his attackers as he did so. He held a grenade but was reluctant to use it for fear of injuring any of the household. Only when the troops retired downstairs did he throw it over the stairs and into the hall below. It failed to explode. More firing from Ernie resulted in Áine O'Rahilly being hit in the face. In *The Singing Flame* O'Malley described his feelings when this accident happened, but Sighle Humphreys was adamant about Ernie not realising that one of his bullets had injured her aunt and the family never making it known to him.

According to that book, it was at this stage only that

Ernie began to fire on the national troops outside in an attempt to make an escape bid through the back garden. Here there was quite a gun battle for a few minutes during which Ernie O'Malley was hit a number of times and seriously wounded. He was bleeding heavily as he was dragged back into the house. He was taken to Baggot Street Hospital; Áine was removed also. The household were told they were under arrest, but Mrs Humphreys insisted on all having breakfast first — including the officer arresting them! Furthermore, she telephoned Madame O'Rahilly to come over and look after the house while they were away. Madame mounted her bicycle and sped to their assistance, but she was arrested also. Meanwhile another raid took place back at Herbert Park where Mary MacSwiney was apprehended. Quite a party of resilient women were lodged in Mountjoy that day.

Outside Humphreys' home, one of the raiding party, Private Peter McCartney from the Curragh Camp, a former member of the Scottish Brigade, was seriously wounded. He died shortly after admission to Baggot Street Hospital.

The de Valera connection with the raid may have arisen because Dick Humphreys wore glasses and was fairly tall. At any rate, he was taken to the bottom of the garden and interrogated — even threatened with shooting, it has been alleged. Only when a Garda Keelan from Donnybrook Station was called to identify Dick for his captors, did they release him.

Documents from the concealed room were being removed to army wagons. Madge Clifford had always looked after security of documents, so on this, as on previous occasions, no vitally important papers were captured.

Earnán Ó Máille was the signature most used on papers which originated from the office of the assistant chief-of-staff. The taking of Castlepollard by the anti-Treaty vice-commandant in Mullingar and thirty men was reported upon, as well as the arrangements for the re-structuring of the Fifth Northern Divison. Here again are the explicit instructions, the crisp, professional approach to soldiering.

Letters from Liam Lynch throw a particular light on the chief-of-staff of the anti-Treaty forces. On 3 August 1922 he wrote to O'Malley from Fermoy:

> Would there be any chance that Free State or British magazines could be located and captured or destroyed in Dublin. Or the place where 18 pounder shells are stored. If these were destroyed it would have the effect of compelling the British to bring them in and hand them over openly — in addition to the actual loss of material. Of course they are already doing this, but the effect would be good.

On 1 October 1922 Lynch wrote:

> I fear you listen to too many soft yarns from these country officers.

And later:

> The squandering of money by those fellows in England should definitely be checked.

Evidently O'Malley was still having the trouble experienced in the Truce period when he himself wrote:

> Officers' accounts will have to be more thoroughly scrutinised in future. NO officer is entitled to spend money on clothes without direct sanction from myself. This, to my mind, unnecessary expense must stop at once, otherwise expenses will have to be met by officers themselves.

Imagine the frustration of the assistant adjutants in O'Malley's command when, on 24 October, they received instructions to submit a diary of activities in each battalion area 'retrospective as from the attack on the courts'. A period of four months! The ACS also wanted full reports of these activities.

A file of British Weekly Intelligence Reports (CR.2/203) was later accorded a note in which a District Inspector recommended that the British authorities should be approached concerning its capture. The commander-in-chief of the national army, however, appended the memo: 'As the British are clearing, the question of their being advised does not arise.' Within the file is a 'SECRET' intelligence report of 24th (P) Infantry Brigade, which incorporates its weekly intelligence summary for seven days ending 26 August 1922, the week of the Michael Collins shooting. It read as follows:

> The tragic death of Michael Collins following so closely on that of Arthur Griffith will probably have one of two effects: it will either cause the army and the nation to lose its temper and take really drastic action against the rebels or it will dishearten them to a dangerous degree.
>
> For the moment the indications are that the second alternative is supervening. P.G. [Provisional Government] Officers at NORTH WALL on the night of the arrival of the late General COLLINS' body were very despondent in their remarks, noticeably lacked any mention of determination to avenge his death. A reliable civilian said that he knew of a woman formerly of strong Republican sympathies who now openly advocated the resumption of control by HM Government and he himself said that people of the middle and professional classes were tired of the unsettled conditions, that they would support the Free State wholeheartedly as long as it could carry on but that when and if it collapsed they would implore the English to come back. He said that ALDERMAN COSGROVE, *(sic)* though a capable and sincere man, would not be able to carry through by himself the task of establishment of order, and it was becoming increasingly difficult to see where new leaders were to be found. These remarks are the more significant as they were made by a man who has hitherto and in the blackest times been firmly confident of the Free State.

There followed a considerable amount of detail about the funeral before the report concluded:

> It has been heard from several sources that a party of secret service men have been told off to shoot DE

VALERA and the idea is to do it in such a way that the blame will fall on some of his own officers.

ROYAL BARRACKS
DUBLIN.

CHB Barnes Capt.
for Col. Commandant
Commanding 24th (P) Inf. Bde.

The valiant and daring Ernie O'Malley had suffered wounds from which he was never to recover fully. When he was transferred to Portobello Barracks from Baggot Street his spirit had gone and he was a pitiful sight. Thomas Gerrard of Ballinstraw, Gorey, an army medical orderly, wrote a letter to him in 1956 recalling his admission. The letter is held in Ernie's papers preserved in University College Dublin archives. In part, it says: 'I counted about sixteen or seventeen wounds in your back. Your smile compelled me to say a few quiet prayers for you.' But O'Malley was soon showing signs of recovery, for a few days later he gave that orderly a note to deliver to Jim Ryan at Fitzwilliam Square. Gerrard said, 'My mind was made up to deliver that note faithfully and all the guns that were previously around the Four Courts would not stop me.' The same orderly attended to a 'whittle' on Erskine Childers' finger the day before his execution.

Execution might well have been O'Malley's lot but for his poor condition. A week before the Childers' execution, on 17 November four other anti-Treaty men died in front of a firing squad in Kilmainham.

On 27 November the chief-of-staff of the anti-Treaty forces wrote to the speaker of the Provisional Government stating that the 'illegal body' over which he [the Speaker] presided, had declared war 'on the soldiers of the Republic and suppressed the legitimate Parliament of the Irish Nation.' There were charges of army brutality towards anti-Treaty prisoners, 'make-believe' trials, murder and transportation, before the letter concluded with a threat:

We therefore give you and each member of your body due notice that unless your army recognises the rules of warfare in the future we shall adopt very drastic measures to protect our forces.

The Provisional Government's reaction was swift and strong. Preparations were made for more executions. The conflict was reaching its acme in bitterness. Joking about the probability of his own death, Ernie O'Malley once quipped that a little more lead one way or the other would not make much difference. Then Seán Hales was shot dead by anti-Treaty forces and, in reprisal, Liam Mellows, Rory O'Connor, Dick Barrett and Joe McKelvey were shot in Mountjoy on 8 December.

As if to suggest the irony of his levity, Ernie O'Malley was moved to Mountjoy for Christmas. He was in a state of agitation and he was still suffering severely from his wounds. He played chess with Bob Barton, fell out with the chaplain, but befriended the governor, Philip Cosgrave, brother of W. T. Cosgrave. A man of humanity, he was concerned about O'Malley's fate and was alleged to have passed out a written message and received back a reply for him.

Peadar O'Donnell, one of Ernie's staunch defenders, re-marked that O'Malley always appeared to have influential acquaintances. In *The Gates Flew Open* Peadar mentioned that the Mountjoy doctors kept insisting that Ernie could not be moved even for a court martial. Sighle Humphreys agreed that they were probably playing for time in order to avert his conviction and execution.

O'Malley's charge sheets were delivered to him. He was accused of waging war, killing a soldier of the national army and other technical offences. 'The evidence accused me of fighting from behind Sheila Humphreys,' he wrote in *The Singing Flame*. Ernie refused to see a solicitor. It was then, perhaps, that his flair for writing first manifested itself. He began to correspond with his family and gave details of his escapades in both wars. The new year dragged on but there was no sign of a court martial for Ernie O'Malley. Outside, there occurred the notorious Bally-seedy incident in which nine anit-Treaty personnel were tied to a log which was then exploded by a mine. Monsignor Luzio visited Cardinal Logue at the Pope's behest. His mission was to obtain first-hand information about events in Ireland but he became involved in peace negotiations besides. In the Nire valley, Waterford, on 24 March, the executive of the anti-Treaty forces met. Eamon de Valera, Liam Lynch, Tom Derrig, Austin Stack, Seán Dowling, Frank Aiken, Bill Quirke, Tom Barry, Tom Crofts, Humphrey Murphy and Seán MacSwiney were there. A notebook of Frank Aiken shows that Ernie O'Malley was still considered a member. Had he been present he would have had little patience with the tales of doom portending the end of the struggle.

Soon after, Tom Derrig was captured and Liam Lynch too. Lynch was severely injured and died shortly after on 10 April 1923. More shootings at Tuam preceded the order from De Valera and Frank Aiken (then chief-of-staff):

> In order to give effect to the decision of the Government and Army Council embodied in the attached proclamation, you will arrange the suspension of all offensive operations in your unit from April 30.

The proclamation once more asserted the sovereign rights of the nation and the maxim that all authority derives from the people.

The order was to take effect not later than 30 April. Liam Deasy said: 'We had experienced ten months of Ireland's greatest tragedy and now at the end, in my opinion, 99% of those responsible on both sides would breathe a fervent "Thank God" while almost all of the people throughout the country would reiterate words of thanks and relief.'*

Seán Dowling said, many years later: 'The Civil War should never have been fought. It was largely caused by Cathal Brugha and his pathological hatred and jealousy of Collins.'

Sighle Humphreys expressed regret that the war caused the demise of the Irish language. Mulcahy and Béaslaí were determined to bring it back as the spoken language, she said many years later. Furthermore they and others had arranged to take the northern counties. And, of course, socialism lost out as a result of the war too, she contended.

* *Brother against Brother*, Mercier Press, 1982, p. 126.

Back in Mountjoy, Ernie O'Malley was depressed, but he soon got down to studying literature, planning escapes and learning Greek — from a Kerryman! His theatrical interests were displayed when he participated in the staging of a satirical pageant.

He was put forward as a candidate for North Dublin in the general election of August 1923, and he was returned as Sinn Féin TD for the constituency, one of the eighteen prisoners elected. He expressed amusement at the fact that Richard Mulcahy's second preference votes won the seat for him.

Fellow prisoners were glad to write in his autograph book: *'Líonn sós cupán cóir, líon dorais deoch na gaedail, agus téascimid an corn ór le ceile?'*

*Seo mar a scriobh Diarmuid Ó Murcadha ó Baile Caislan Bheara, Corcaigh.* Paddy Mahon of Offaly No. 2 Brigade wrote:

There was a young maid from Japan
She married an African man.
    She was quite yellow
    And he a nice follow
And the kiddles are all Black and Tans.

Ernie's brother Cecil signed. Eighteen-year-old Patrick was a prisoner too. J. Gibbons of Enniscorthy wrote literary entries followed by 'Up Dev'.

In *Survivors,* Con Casey told of an occasion when hoses were used on prisoners and they were roughly treated after having 'an almighty row' with the prison authorities. He claimed that this brought about the long hunger strike which began in October. Ernie O'Malley disapproved of the strike. The realist in him regarded it as obsolete, since it had failed to win anything for Terence MacSwiney except posthumous glory. As a mark of solidarity, however, he began the ordeal with the others. In *The Gates Flew Open,* Peadar O'Donnell described a dying George Plunkett and a severely ill O'Malley chuckling over a cookery book during the ordeal. These men were removed to Kilmainham shortly after the strike began. Ernie became progressively weaker so that he was anointed. A visit from his own family doctor brought him the warning that he could do himself permanent injury by continuing without food. After one death the strike ended, having lasted forty-one days. As one of the strikers was said to have remarked, 'We beat Christ by a day!'

Another Christmas in jail, after which a number of prisoners were removed to the Curragh. Ernie, still in a deplorable condition, was admitted to St Bricin's General Military Hospital off Infirmary Road where he was operated upon. Then he went to the Curragh hospital where he heard tales about the 'Tobin Mutiny' which was fomenting among army officers. A letter to President Cosgrave, dated 6 March 1924 and signed by Major General Liam Tobin and Colonel Charles Dalton, demanded a conference with government representatives to discuss the interpretation of the Treaty as envisaged by the IRA. An order was issued for the arrest of the signatories and others. As a result, acts of a mutinous nature occurred.

Ernie was soon well enough to be moved to the internment camp known as 'Tintown'. There were few officers in his hut and he relished the stories of hardship told by the men. Another autograph:

*Is treise an ceart ná an bpreab is mó*

*Brian Ó hUigínn*
*Currach Chille Dara.*

O'Malley participated in organising dramas, musical recitals and, of course, musketry lectures. More escapes were planned, but Ernie was not involved in any actual breaks. He was released from custody on 24 July 1924.

# 5

# Wanderings and Worries

*He said, 'My Royal Mistress*
*Sends her men-at-arms and me*
*With greetings good to all her friends*
*Who true and loyal be.*
*Her liegeman, Lord Hal Sydney*
*With all his spears awaits*
*For you to open wide to him*
*The Barbican and gates!'*

The Oath of Allegiance laid down in Article 4 of the Treaty and Article 17 of the Constitution of 1922 was anathema to Ernie O'Malley so there was no question of his taking his seat in the Dáil. On 21 October, Aibhistín dí Staic and Seoirse Ó Dálaigh, secretaries of Sinn Féin, wrote from 23 Suffolk Street, Dublin, informing Ernie of his nomination for the positions of vice-president and honorary treasurer of the organisation. Twelve thousand members had been interned, so that there were considerable tensions prevailing. O'Malley was still a young, if injured, man at twenty seven years-of-age. He and his family felt that he needed a complete break, so he decided to go abroad for a short while.

From this point in his life, the Ernie O'Malley story became a nightmare for future researchers. He kept little contact with family or friends but was inclined to wander away alone — often for considerable spells. Few would ever know where he went or what he did. Some of his activities came to light after persistent searchings but to lay them down in a concise chronological manner often depended upon bits and scraps of evidence. Some of this was in his own handwriting which was most difficult to dicipher.

However, everyone who was in occasional contact with him during the period stresses the fact that he was a very sick man, that he still carried around bullets in him and that he was almost a nervous wreck.

Journeyings in the south of France evoked his approving comment on the brick architecture of Toulouse, especially its fine Romanesque cathedral, as well as regrets about being unable to remain longer in places which attracted him. Then he was off through Saint Lizier to St Gironds, on a train to Sentein or a trip across the border to Pico Schrader in Spain; then to Barcelona, where he noted being employed in some consular office.

Italy, too, stirred his love for the arts again, and praise for Florentine art, appraisals of Massacio, Fra' Angelico. He would write a quick note about a particular sculpture or a long paragraph about a pleasant church nave. His eye captured beauty wherever he roamed and on return visits he wrote about particularly pleasing aspects.

But if the main purpose in Ernie's trip to the continent was his recovery, he was not content to sit about and get well. As his colleagues back home were meeting in the Rotunda to record their protest against the tripartite agreement between the United Kingdom, Northern Ireland and the Irish Free State — some articles of which consolidated partition — Ernie O'Malley was climbing the Pyrenees and the Italian hills. Climbing was a remarkable feat for a man in his poor physical condition. Indeed, he had special shoes made for the purpose by a cobbler in the tiny village of Bourgmdain.

Perhaps he was testing his mettle before he embarked on another adventure, this time on the Franco–Spanish border. This vital red-head had tasted adventure, and while he was suffering in body and in spirit for what he regarded as a lost dream, there were others to welcome the voice of guerrilla experience.

Since the seventeenth century the Catalonian region of north-east Spain had seen revolt, cross-border incursions and full-scale invasions. In 1697, Barcelona was taken by Louis XIV of France but was returned to Spain by the

Treaty of Rijswijk (1697). Home rule was eventually granted to Catalonia, the Basque lands and Galicia. Indeed, since 1977 they have their own flags. Catalonia's is yellow, with red horizontal stripes.* Ernie O'Malley had a part in the region's history and it was with the approval of the IRA executive that he visited the Catalonians during his European sojourn. His spirited exhortations led to an escapade which had all the ingredients of a musical comedy plot.

Seán MacBride had escaped from detention when being moved from Mountjoy to Kilmainham in 1923. Technically, he was still on the run when Ernie O'Malley visited him in Paris in 1925. As always, he remained a while and disappeared without a word of explanation.

Seán had close contacts with the French police because of British secret service raids on his home. The Parisian police knew about these and reluctantly tolerated them. They did not like them taking place within their jurisdiction, however, so they asked Seán if he wished to have them stopped. He agreed and they did not occur again. Seán also had contact with the French army and the Catalonians, including Colonel Macia who later became president of the Catalan Republic.

The house-guest had been gone a while but returned in time to take a trip to Brittany with the MacBrides. On their return to Paris, Ernie again disappeared, but this time Seán heard about his movements. He had been arrested in Italy for possession of a dagger. Seán used his influence with the French authorities to have him returned to his care. His house-guest looked unwell and acted in an erratic manner. One morning he was missing again.

Weeks later a member of the French army intelligence service called to the MacBride home. He said he had information about O'Malley helping the Catalans in planning an invasion of Spain from the French side. He hoped Seán would prevail on him to desist. Seán travelled to meet Colonel Macia who was enthusiastic about the O'Malley inspired plan. Provisions had been made for the com-

* *Flags of the World*, E. M. C. Barraclough, London: Frederick Warne.

mandeering of a train for the following Saturday. This would take thirty to forty Catalans at full steam to the Spanish border, across which they would launch a sortie.

Colonel Macia was disappointed at MacBride discouraging the idea. 'Did you discuss the cancellation with General O'Malley?' he demanded to know. Seán admitted not having seen Ernie and had great difficulty in talking the colonel out of continuing with his invasion.

Scarcely a month later the raid was planned again; and again, French army intelligence called on MacBride to defuse the situation. However, the operation did eventually take place. The train was commandeered. Ernie O'Malley and his Catalan friends were on board giving advice to the enthusiastic raiders, but they were halted by the French before the border was reached.

Then there was the O'Malley connection with the Mediterranean province of Morocco known as Er Rif. The area embraces the central part of the Rif mountains where Abd-El-Krim had achieved fame for spearheading resistance to the implantation of the Spanish protectorate. He had routed a Spanish force of 20,000 strong in 1921 and had then established a rudimentary state under his own organisation and leadership. In 1925 French forces pushed from the south penetrating the Wargla valley. Abd-El-Krim counter-attacked and almost reached Fez, but his success sparked off a combined Franco-Spanish reaction. Spanish forces landed at Alhucemas while Marshal Petain led 160,00 French from the south.

It is generally believed that Ernie O'Malley was in close contact with Abd-El-Krim, but the elusive knight-errant left even less trace of his movements than usual. He was in the Rif mountains at one period during 1925, so it is not unlikely that he became involved in the Rif resistance. His brother, Albert, died in 1925 having contracted Blackwater Fever in Nigeria.

Luke Malley did not suffer inactivity lightly and when his wandering son returned from the continent he prevailed upon him to attempt taking up his medical studies where he had left off eight years earlier. After all, Cecil was now a qualified doctor, Kevin was completing his medical studies and Paddy was in a good banking position.

Ernie O'Malley returned to University College Dublin in the autumn of 1926. He was older and more experienced than the other students in his year. Here was a fusing of outlooks and a search for new outlets to speed recovery from a turbulent and exciting set of experiences. In a November letter to Frank Gallagher, he noted that he was trying to work hard.*

The college's Saturday night debates featured prominent figures like Frank Ryan, who had graduated a year earlier, and Tom O'Rourke. Ernie O'Malley was an enthusiastic attender. He joined with these, Roger McHugh, Florrie Lynch, Michael Farrell, author of *Thy Tears Might Cease,* and others to form a literary coterie within the halls of learning.

John Nash was auditor of the Literary and Historical Society when in March 1928 Ernie and Michael Farrell pressed for the society's involvement in drama. An extraordinary meeting resulted and before long a dramatic club emerged, of which Ernie was first director. It was under the auspices of the Literary and Historical Society and was fully endorsed by it.

Progress was swift and the club's first plays were soon produced. Presidential sanction was received from the progressive Dr Coffey to transform the Aula Maxima in St Stephen's Green — and the building received electric lighting for the first time. Soon the celebrated Dramatic Society (Dramsoc) emerged and commenced an independent existence with a director of its own choosing, Paddy Donovan, to whom Ernie O'Malley handed over stewardship.

Despite the apparent harmony, however, the society's third director, writing later in the *History of the Literary and Historical Society, UCD,* recalled that the president 'rather resisted' the formation of the drama club at first. Robin Dudley Edwards (later Professor) went on to say that its institution 'within and financed by the L. & H.' was considered by Dr Coffey to be the 'thin edge of the student

* Frank Gallagher Papers, National Library.

wedge'. The group, led by O'Malley, acquitted itself so well, however, that the president rowed in with it.

Some of the Literary and Historical Society members who debated on Saturday nights continued their arguments in the Dublin mountains next day because they were also members of the college walking club who met in the main hall of UCD on Sunday mornings and set off on their ramblings. Ernie defied his limbs that still were weak by joining in the walks with gusto.

Dr Coffey gave Ernie grinds in his medical subjects, but his continuing ill-health, combined with his proliferating interests in artistic and literary pursuits, mitigated against his passing his examinations. Once, when he asked Peadar O'Donnell to read a poem he had written, Peadar replied, 'Save it and read it to your father when you fail your examinations.' He left the university in 1928.

The new Fianna Fáil party broke with the Sinn Féin policy of abstention from Dáil Éireann in August 1927. It entered the Dáil and was soon planning a newspaper which would become its forum. So it was that in 1928 Frank Aiken set off for the United States to raise money for the proposed *Irish Press*. He was accompanied by Ernie O'Malley.

At 4.30 a.m. on Columbus Day, 12 October 1928, O'Malley disembarked from the *George Washington* at New York. His first impressions of *Mundus Novus* were unprofound. There was the ill-mannered passport checker who smoked as he stamped passengers' documents; those not smoking appeared to be chewing gum. He did approve of the advertised fine for spitting: $500. The shop fronts on Fifth Avenue were good to look at, even if the police did appear casual as they jauntily strolled along the sidewalks twirling their batons. Dinner at an Italian restaurant cost a mere dollar. All doors closed automatically, but the city's post-civil-war architecture was ugly, he observed.

Of the Americans with their 'loud, shrill, nasal voices,' Ernie remarked on their having no past, little present but mostly future.* He pronounced that their art was influenced by their business outlook, which was ruthless; it was

* O'Mally Papers, University Collge Dublin Archives.

valued for its price rather than for its beauty. Their conversation lacked spontaneity and he deplored their habit of avoiding the words 'please' and 'thanks'. But he found them kind and anxious to please.

On his first day there, the temperature was 83°F in the shade. He went to Liberty Street and saw the original Republican Bonds. His habit of illustrating his letters first became apparent then. He drew a circular clothes line, a muffin and explained that a 'cookie' was a biscuit.

His papers suggest that he operated initially from an office at Transportation Building, 225 Broadway. He had communications with the Eastern States Professional Schools for Teachers at Press Buildings in Washington Square East and again he had contact with Johnny Raleigh. Entries in his appointments diary for that period suggest that he visited Newark and Jersey City, contacting people previously associated with the Republican Bonds Drive, of which he had a list.

He arrived in Boston where he addressed a meeting of the Central Council of the Irish Country Clubs. A note described the audience as pathetic and a little hostile. A Mayo man attempted to enforce a limit of ten minutes for his talk. He was impressed by the city's architecture and by certain refrigeration systems.

Mark Twain's Connecticut capital Hartford was visited, and upon his return to Boston he noted that he had raised $27,276 to date. Most of this came from persons who had subscribed to Eamon de Valera during his early 1920s drive. Local committees were established to continue the work after his departure.

Philadelphia, Cleveland, Chicago and on to the west coast. He received warm receptions from past members of the American Association for the recognition of the Irish Republic. In April 1929 Frank Aiken returned to Ireland, but Ernie was soon in Berkeley, not then part of San Francisco. He saw Sara Munro on stage there. He had a sitting with the celebrated photographer, Edward Weston, who mistakenly referred to him as 'Shawn O'Malley'.

Meanwhile, Frank Gallagher, who was to edit the *Irish*

*Press,* wrote to Ernie. He related to him how a book of IRA stories called *Challenge of the Sentry* had been published. Ernie figured in it, 'though not by name or other identification'. There was also an introduction to a Jacob Baker of Vanguard Press on New York's Fifth Avenue who would lend him a gun, if he required it. Frank expressed delight at hearing Ernie was writing. 'Don't let anything depress or turn you from it,' he wrote. 'You were made for that more than for anything. Put yourself into what you write,' he advised.*

By June, Ernie was in Los Angeles. A little later, in Pasadena, he met with the Golden family. Peter Golden, who had died three years previously, had lectured extensively on Irish affairs throughout the United States. He was secretary and fund-raiser for a group called the Irish Progressive League. His father, Terence, had taught in Macroom. An tAthair Peadar Ó Laoghaire was one of his pupils. At the behest of Terence MacSwiney's brother Peter and with encouragement from Seán T. Ó Ceallaigh, Peter's body was returned for burial in the Republican Plot of St Finbarr's Cemetery, Cork, the only non-combatant interred there. Peter and his wife Helen, or Merriam, had both been actors with the Ben Greet Company, a travelling group.

Peter's son Terence, a Colorado Springs realtor and former folk-entertainer and teacher at Fountain Valley School there, wrote an article in the college's *Alumni Bulletin*. He described how the family moved to Taos in New Mexico in 1930, mainly because his mother wished 'to escape progress'. The article captured the atmosphere of the expedition and also provided a succinct comment on Ernie O'Malley. (It is reproduced in part, with the author's permission.)

> We drove to the Grand Canyon from Pasadena in the fall of 1929. Mother found this less arduous than she had anticipated. . . so we continued on to Santa Fe. There Mother discovered that an old friend, the Irish poetess, Ella Young, was visiting in Taos; so we drove on up to

* O'Malley Papers, University College Dublin Archives.

Taos. . . and were hooked! We were travelling in a 1925 Chevrolet sedan with all the paraphernalia typical of the day: an extra spare tire and rim roped onto the regular one at the back, bedrolls piled on the roof of the car and more bedrolls tied between the fenders and hood, an expandable rack on the running-board crammed full of gear, a triplet of cans clamped to the running board — white for water, red for gas, and blue for oil — and water bags dangling from the bumpers.

In addition to 'the folks', there was I, age about eleven or twelve and Ernie O'Malley, who had been a commandant-general in the Irish Republican Army at the age of nineteen, or something. Ernie was volatile, fascinating, exciting, entertaining, infuriating, impetuous, brilliant. . .

When we left the Grand Canyon via a terrifying trail called the 'Navahopi Road', Ernie gallantly offered to drive. His credentials as a chauffeur did not inspire confidence; he had a habit of putting his foot on the clutch instead of on the brake. Well, Mother and Mariana [Howes, a friend of the family] were standing on the running boards amongst all the clutter and junk, clinging desperately to the door frames. (I suppose they thought they were lookouts.) I was sitting on the front seat, next to Ernie. We were going down a tortuous pitch of rocks and ruts that made an abrupt right turn at the bottom of an unbelievably steep hill. There was a good reason for the turn. If you missed it, you dropped several hundred feet off a cliff into the canyon of the Little Colorado. Terror and tension mounted. Sure as hell, Ernie hit the clutch instead of the brake. We didn't quite make the turn. The car vaulted a boulder. Mother and Mariana got bounced off into the rocks and cactus. I grabbed what was appropriately called in those days 'the emergency brake', and the car stopped two or three feet this side of Eternity.

Terence Golden's sister Eithne added the remark that Ernie did not volunteer to drive again.

Ella Young then lived in Halcyon, California, and was

visiting in Taos with the wealthy Mabel Dodge Lujan from Buffalo who had married a Pueblo Indian. She was in the habit of inviting people interested in the arts. It was at her behest that D. H. Lawrence and his wife had gone to Taos some years earlier. Mabel was author of a book on Lawrence entitled *Lorenzo in Taos*. Ernie wished to visit Ella Young too. Merriam Golden thought he wished her to assist him in writing his first book *On Another Man's Wound*. Others deny this vehemently and point out that Ella Young had been described as one of the 'slighter poets' who was a disciple of A. E. and who contributed poems and books of Celtic wonder tales to the revival period — despite the American press's description of her as 'the leading poet in Ireland' when she arrived there in 1925 to lecture in Columbia University. Her book *Flowering Duck* (1945) certainly did not make an impact anything like Ernie O'Malley's *On Another Man's Wound*.

The Goldens and Mariana Howes decided to remain in Taos. Ernie appeared to like the place, as he too remained on. He stayed at Adam's Auto Camp, an establishment like today's motel except for the feature elaborated upon by Terence Golden:

> The toilet at Adam's Camp was a sort of communal affair — a big shed with 'women' on one side and 'men' on the other. Each side was a five or six holer. Conversation resounded dramatically throughout the structure. One night the entire camp was awakened by pandemonium erupting from the privy. A bunch of burros had gotten into the women's side.
>
> Before the lead donkey discovered he'd come to a dead end, those behind him were shoving and pushing to get in. They were all braying and bawling and kicking hell out of the privy and very nearly finished it off before they were extricated. Thank heaven there was a good, sound floor. . .
>
> There was no plumbing on our place, no electricity, no phone. We were one of three or four Gringo families within a radius of two miles. Mother didn't want to have

to relocate the privy every year to two, so she decreed that the hole (called officially a 'privy vault') would be ten feet deep. The structure itself was rather palatial; the outside was plastered with adobe to 'harmonise' with the prevailing architecture. Getting the hole dug ten feet deep was the hard part. The local workmen regarded this as utterly absurd; they had never known one to be more than three feet deep. When the hole was two feet deep, they began coming around to see if it was deep enough. Of course the whole crew stopped work while their emissary scouted out someone in authority. These stoppages occurred more frequently as the depth increased. When they finally accepted Mother's determination, someone cut a pole ten feet long, and, with every few inches dug, work would stop while the pole was lowered into the hole to measure accomplishment.

One day O'Malley asked, 'Have you seen the Earl's daughter with puce pants?' And this was how we met the artist, Dorothy Brett. . . she carried an old brass ear trumpet. . . [and] was then wearing those long, baggy, corduroy French peasants' pants of a purplish colour ('puce' to those raised in England or Ireland).

In his book on D. H. Lawrence entitled *Portrait of a Genius but.* . . . Richard Aldington told how Dorothy Brett followed after the celebrated author, to the displeasure of his wife Frieda. He also told how Mabel Lujan gave her 170 acre Lobo ranch (seventeen miles from Taos) to Frieda and how Lawrence preferred that remote place to 'the smart house' at Taos. Dorothy Brett's cabin was beside it. Terence Golden remarked: 'Everyone in Taos who thought he was anybody in the field of the arts appointed himself a surrogate for the salvation of Lawrence's soul.'

Some commentators put Ernie into that category, but his love for Taos and his interest in its cultures absorbed him then. When the Goldens made a trip back to Pasadena he remained on to work on his manuscript. On their return, they moved into a cabin near the auto-camp and Ernie visited them regularly to read his work to Merriam and Mariana. Eithne Golden Sax remembered hearing him read passages about the Four Courts, which would suggest that his writing covered what eventually emerged as two books, *On Another Man's Wound* and *The Singing Flame*. She also recalled a visit to Acoma Pueblo when they were starting down a steep trail and, in an impetuous moment of fun, Ernie grabbed her and whirled her along as he ran hastily down.

Early in 1930 further negotiations brought the Goldens back to Pasadena yet again. The author Spud Johnson was also leaving for a while so Ernie moved into his adobe house. Ernie brandished his pen and notebook again — this time to write down household hints passed on by Mrs Golden. Some suggest that the housekeeping was not successful and that he moved into Dorothy Brett's. This is unlikely, but he did go there to ride the Honourable Dorothy's horses. Ella Young noted how he endured great pain in trying to ride, but he persisted and overcame his difficulties.

The daughter of an English peer, the Viscount of Esker, was an unlikely friend for Ernie, but Dorothy had few imperialistic traits. Lawrence thought her 'a little simple but harmless', but the Indians in Taos said of her, 'Señorita with dagger very dangerous'. Mabel Lujan thought her a 'holy Russian idiot'. She later published *Lawrence and Brett*.

About this time Ernie attempted to climb a rock peak above the Salto — the waterfall said to have been the locale in Lawrence's *The Woman Who Rode Away*. He took a bad fall and injured his back and ankle. He lay alone for a number of hours unable to move. His relentless fight against the effects of his wounds and tortures continued.

His friendship with the Goldens continued on their return to settle in Taos. He particularly liked Merriam's pear-chip jam and the come-as-you-please atmosphere of her household, but he was bitten by the wanderlust again and left around June 1930. More notes marked his departure. They were for the three Golden children, advising them on things like learning inward gaiety and

outward repose from the Indians. A little humour was
included too; harking back to his chiding one of them
for taking a sponge bath in the sink, he wrote: 'Don't
wash your feet in the sink — the sink has feelings too!'

An elaborate system of note-keeping was a feature of
all Ernie's compilations and research. He used a type of
code *viz:*

●   on visit.

x ☐   name repeated on page.

☐   died since last seen

(   ) . notebook in which notes taken as man talked

[   ]   notebook into which notes transcribed

His entries included aspects of life among the Indians; to
some of them he was 'their amigo'. Their life styles, forms
of government, festivals and landscapes, irrigation systems, cultivation, poisonous plants and fruits were all
noted — Aztec ceremonies and flower markets too. More
advanced development of his ideas were obvious in drafts
of essays on the *United States South West and Mexico,* in
seven parts. There were allusions to sports like pole-climb-
ing and relay races. He liked their dance routines with their
sensuous rhythms to 'riot the blood', but he wondered was
there something evil about being caught up in their
atmosphere. Pueblo Indians, Mexicans — whatever the
race, Ernie displayed a lively passionate interest in their
origins, customs and cultures.

Always there was notational material for his *magnum
opus:* the Limerick agreement between Liam Lynch and
Michael Brennan before the Civil War; the possibility of
handing over arms to anti-Treaty troops by Mulcahy for
use in the north; the activities of the IRB prior to the signing of the Treaty and their subsequent procedure up to and
after the vote on acceptance of the Treaty; Wilson's work
and career in the north or in connection with the north; a
memory of Rory O'Connor's posting up the proclamation
in the Four Courts. Random notes on random thoughts.
Questions too: What was the motive behind the Wilson
assassination?

Mexico was a change from New Mexico, but on his way

there he remarked on the slow rate of work among road workers. He had been warned that the country would be over-run by tourists but noted that if the roads were ever completed to get them in they would still be lost in its vastness. Train timetables were erratic. If there was a hint that some tourists might turn up at the station, the train would wait hours. Bandits stripped wealthy visitors — even of their socks.

Ernie displayed a keen humour in describing a quest for the W.C. in a hotel. The dining-room basin was offered but he thought there were too many people present! Then the kitchen sink, but 'the cooks were Indian and a little shy.' The manager finally shouted, '*Excusado*', and brought Ernie to the lavatory. He was so effusively polite that Ernie thought he would remain to pull the chain. He also felt that any race calling these things an *excusado* was genteel and that name also described the country — '*excusado*'.

A retired British army officer tried to make contact with Ernie while he was in Mexico. He claimed to have resigned from the army in protest against the Black and Tan atrocities. His constant reference to Ernie as 'Commandant-General' annoyed him till he remarked to a friend, 'Did you ever smell a secret service man? The poor British still (pardon me, Señora) think they are like their own backsides — they can't be licked.'

One of Ernie's 'Lettertoons' — mixtures of text and drawing — emanated from Mexico. It was created between courses as he dined with the artist Dorothy Stewart. In it he bears a remarkable resemblance to James Joyce. Dorothy and Theodora Goddard of New York were his escorts in Mexico and he stayed for a while with Hart Crane, the American poet who wrote the celebrated work on Brooklyn Bridge called *The Bridge*. He studied at Mexico City University of the Arts and taught in regional high schools. Being in rural areas allowed him to meet Indians and mestizos in over a dozen states. He lectured a bit on Anglo-Irish literature.

He loved what he was doing and his skin took on a healthier look. He was not even perturbed about losing four chapters of his manuscript. During one visit to a theatre he noted that girls' slit dresses showed 'a foot and a half of belly' as they swung vigorously to display their tiny little tights. But he also remarked on dignified women with oval faces, dressed in black and singing almost in a Russian manner. Men sang in the street — to harp accompaniment. And the native-carved statues of Adam and Eve had such large fig leaves!

There was some border-hopping at this time, for he spent some time in the Spanish-speaking village of Chimayo, about fifty miles south of Taos. The place was renowned for its brilliantly coloured striped blankets and boasted an old adobe church, the Santuario. Merriam Golden, her daughter, Mariana Howes and others visited him there and he brought Merriam to listen to the beautiful singing and organ playing of a Catalan priest who had befriended Ernie because of his familiarity with the homeland.

The ladies slept on the floor of Ernie's hired adobe house and he played host at breakfast. He had no cooker, but the rent was a mere $5 a month. Presiding over breakfast prepared on a trivet by a corner fireplace, his cuisine depended on a knife, fork, spoon, coffee-pot and frying pan. Mrs Golden must have admired how he had benefited from her notes!

The oldest capital in the United States, founded by the Spaniards in 1610, found Ernie's approval too. In Santa Fe he was reported to have visited the family of Brian Boru Dunn who was editor of the *Santa Fe New Mexican*. But the most interesting reports were those about his alleged illegal re-entry into the United States.

His visa had expired and there were suggestions that the Saorstat Éireann government let it be known to United States immigration authorities that his return to Ireland was undesirable. They might be watching out for him, therefore. He swam the Rio Grande or otherwise pulled the wool over the authorities' eyes by surreptitiously straying across among a flock of sheep. Those were the standard folkore versions. Dorothy Brett was not satisfied with their lack of flamboyance, so she had Ernie swimming across the river among a flock of sheep with his clothes bound to his head. When Merriam Golden told Ernie she was dying to know the real story he merely grinned, 'Well, you can keep on dying.'

In December 1930, Peadar O'Donnell had written to Frank Gallagher concerning Ernie O'Malley's suitability to edit the literary page of his 'new paper'. 'The content of Ernie's mind qualifies him beyond all others I know,' he said. Not knowing where Ernie was, he added, 'He might not be so trail-less that he could not be located.' Peadar did trace him — through Kevin Malley — and was soon pleased to be able to inform Frank that Ernie was not only keen, 'but would be disappointed if the thing' did not come off.*

Frank expressed the fear that Ernie might be thought 'unsteady'. This reference came about because of whispered rumours which began to hover about creamy pints in Dublin and which spread like seeded dandelions to proliferate in various places around the globe.

*The Irish Press* was launched in September 1931 — without O'Malley as literary editor. The Goldens in Taos, however, got an unexpected surprise. The red-haired raconteur who had vowed never to return came back among them. He immediately enlisted the aid of the children in segregating his memoirs within his adobe which they called the 'mouse house' — because the heat brought out the smell of rodents. Indeed they often sat in their overcoats rather than light the stove. The children's studies had long been neglected so he announced that his adobe would be a classroom for Terence, Deirdre and Eithne. Mrs Golden gave him board in return for his tutorials. She was glad of the arrangement because Taos High School was Spanish-speaking and had a limited curriculum. Indeed, it closed altogether eventually because of underfunding brought about by the depression. It was then that a shy Spanish-speaking native girl named Aurora joined Ernie's 'academy', the wall of which bore a large-scale operational map from his guerrilla days in Ireland. Eithne Golden Sax

* Frank Gallagher Papers, National Library.

remembered, as did Seán Dowling many years later, how Ernie was in the habit of scribbling comments on books. Her recollection was of a chastisement on *A Walk in Hellas* by Denton Snyder: 'Oh, shadow of Denton J. Snyder, why didn't you include a map — and a good one.'

Ernie taught up to six subjects, including Spanish, English grammar, history and mathematics, plus a little art history and appreciation. Eithne Golden Sax remembered the peculiarity of his speaking Spanish with a distinct Irish accent, as well as occasional mispronunciations of English. As he taught, he improved his own Spanish, learned while in Spain. Deirdre Golden remembered how Ernie could 'be so funny'. On one occasion when she got Julius Caesar mixed up with Paul Revere, he roared with laughter. Shakespeare readings were frequently held.

From Elie Faure's *History of Art* he read at great speed. The children had to write down what he spoke. Previously, they had only learned to print their letters, so this exercise had the added purpose of practising them in longhand. Writings of the German philosopher, Arthur Schopenhauer, who believed that man's irrational will was the only reality, were not guaranteed to hold the interest of such young students — particularly Aurora. 'Hell, that stuff had a narcoleptic effect on us, let alone poor Aurora,' recalled Terence Golden. Yet Ernie displayed great patience with the 'little lassie'. He planned a particular curriculum for her and he encouraged her gently, whereas he was inclined to bully the Goldens. Deirdre remembered his saying, 'You're the most ignorant people I've ever known.'

A typical day started with the children lighting the stove and boiling water for Ernie's tea which he insisted on making himself so 'that you could trot a mouse on it.' When the water was ready they would move away to feed the horses and the dog, Mullingar — so named by Mariana Howes who declared, 'He's a big, black, fuzzy animal and it (Mullingar) sounds a big, black, fuzzy name.' The dog may also have been given the name because of Ernie's disagreement with the monument there back in the twenties (see page 42).

At one stage during 1932, Mrs Golden was admitted to hospital in Santa Fe with pneumonia. Ernie took complete charge and ran the family's daily lives as if they were soldiers under his command. He held a type of conference each evening and planned 'time sheets' for the next day. 'Orderlies' were appointed to place matches in a small Indian pottery container, to fill condiment sets, replenish supplies and assist him with cooking and cleaning.

Progress was checked and spare time accounted for next day — in writing! 'Fifteen minutes looking for a lost nail-file' was strongly criticised. Terence Golden remembered Ernie writing by the light of a kerosene lamp in the room next to his. Right into the night he worked, talking occasionally to the dog and feeding it crackers.

There was time for relaxation too — the 'Fianna boar hunts', for example. In accordance with a New Mexican custom, its Spanish-speaking population turned their livestock loose on St Francis' Day, to be cared for by the saint, it was supposed. The hungry beasts wandered about in search of food, and pigs often invaded Golden's orchard. Ernie organised the fashioning of 'spears' from willow rods and engaged the services of Dorothy Stewart's bull-hound 'Cochiti' for the game in which the swine were hunted from the orchard and across the countryside. The dog sometimes grabbed a sow's ear and got whisked along in mid-air — a Pueblo *Bran* or *Sceolan,* for 'Cochiti' is the name of a New Mexican pueblo. Ernie rode *Macha,* Mrs Golden's big, black, twenty-dollar mare.

Sometimes they would have a picnic when Ernie's surprise delicacy would be fried bread, beloved everyday diet of Irish children then, but considered a special treat by his 'Fianna'. Like that body, there were tests of members' mettle. One day Ernie had them line up their ponies to block his progress as he thundered towards them on *Macha*. Eithne's little mare, called *Ciotóg,* did what its name implied and turned left. Deirdre's swung off to the right and *Macha* with her rider charged through. O'Malley did not approve of the lack of nerve among his young female cavalry. However, from the severity there came breaking through signs of a sensitive and gentle inner being. One night an outhouse roof or straw rack collapsed, causing Deirdre to cry in fear at the noise. Many years afterwards she remembered Ernie's kindly concern when he dashed to her room to console her. When Eithne's mare died of colic he displayed great sympathy with the over-wrought child.

There was also the lively side of things — teaching the children to sing *Whack-fol-de-diddle* or reciting nonsense verse, as when Eithne had a cold and he was moved to com-pose:

> Eithne's nose is red,
> And Eithne's nose is long;
>    'Twould be no disgrace
>    To Eithne's face,
> If Eithne's nose was gone.

Evening readings might be from Samuel Butler's 1872 satire on contemporary life, *Erewhon*. On one occasion he invited Emil Bisttram, a painter, and his wife for dinner. The 'duties' of his 'staff' were augmented that day as the living room was tidied up and cushions rearranged because the guests had an eye for colour.

The Goldens were amused by idioms common to Ireland but novel to them. They thought the dog was being com-mended for bravery having done something wrong when Ernie said, 'You're a very bold dog'. They sang dumb when he had one of his outbursts: telling them that they listened with their feet, that they were show-offs laying on the use of big words or that they just wanted to 'trot out' something they had picked up.

Once, refusing an invitation to visit a friend, he sent the children along with a note saying he wasn't coming but he was sending 'three artillery', two heavy and one light — this because Deirdre and Eithne were incessant talkers but Terence somewhat quieter. Deirdre remembered giving Ernie a playful slap on the back one day and his wincing with the pain, but not being angry with her.

He gave the family comic-book Indian names. Merriam

was Squaw Gnaw-the-Pouch of the Kick-in-the-Pants tribe. There was Chief Spit-in-the-Wind and Chief Sit-in-the-Car too. Similar methods were used by him, he claimed, to instruct his Fianna Éireann company and his brothers back in Dublin. He held that when the imagination and communal sense were stimulated it was easier to talk about attitudes and quality of life than if it were done in a preaching, classroom situation.

The recollections of the Golden family suggest that this period of Ernie O'Malley's life brought him most fulfilment. He was possibly happiest in that artists' colony. Imparting knowledge and instilling discipline and routine in a household which had previously enjoyed a glorious disorganisation pleased him. And he knew when to stop, for he discontinued the chart-keeping when he noticed signs of over-organisation appearing. Yet Eithne Golden Sax tried ever after to organise her life — to be her 'own Ernie O'Malley'. Her meticulous tabulation of points for this part of the Ernie O'Malley story bore testimony of her success. Her own words provide an apt conclusion to the New Mexico connection:

It was a sad occasion all around when the time came for him to leave — he was obviously moved. . . Again, as when he left Taos the first time, he left written words of wisdom for us children. All I remember is something about keeping our lives organised, but not letting things get over-organised to the point where 'organisation eats itself' . . . We never saw him again. . .

*[Ernie O'Malley's movements throughout his stay in America and Mexico are not securely established. Conflict exists between sources and so reasonable assumptions have been made where discrepancies have been noted.]*

In March 1932 Fianna Fáil came to power and formed a government with de Valera as Taoiseach. Frank Aiken was minister for defence and it is sometimes said that he contacted Ernie O'Malley with a view to his returning to Ireland to accept the position of assistant chief-of-staff in the army (confirmation for which could not be obtained from the late Mr Aiken). A more likely suggestion says that librarianship at the department of defence was on offer.

Unemployment was rife in the United States during that year and a popular song of the period was *Brother, Can You Spare a Dime.* Franklin D. Roosevelt was elected President on 8 November and he created federal agencies to deal with the pervasive crisis and try to bring the country out of the recession. It was an arduous time for Ernie O'Malley to arrive in New York. He stayed a while with a Boston lawyer, John T. Hughes, where he wrote part of his book.

Out of work, he was nonetheless welcome in society circles but his socialising was reluctant. He endured it to eat. Ever eager to capitalise on trivia, receptions buzzed with tales of his eccentricity. His friends claimed this was in retaliation for the outspoken way he told people exactly what he thought of them.

Shyness and tension exaggerated minor nervous problems, still provoked by his physical condition. A friend remarked how his ankle could be circled by his thumb and forefinger, almost. There was an air of awe among socialites towards this man who had been a general in the struggle for Irish freedom — and 'at only twenty years-of-age' they erroneously declared.

On a visit to an upstate artists' colony at Yaddo he made friends with people of assorted backgrounds. He continued a deep artistic association with them during the remainder of his stay in America, enjoying a stimulating intellectual and artistic transience.

In the city, he visited art galleries and museums. Stories circulated about his leadership at home which extended beyond his troops to his 'office of adoring lady secretaries on the *qui vive,* besides.' There were disclosures that he paid no gallantry or chivalry towards women — only a hearty sort of comradeship. One commentator said, 'Of course, Ernie is peculiarly ascetic. I would not be surprised if he took orders some day, as he is half monk already.'

One of his first visits to the Hooker family of Greenwich, Connecticut occurred about then. According to his son, Cormac, Maraquita Villard brought him down in June. These were wealthy people who also had rich friends. Blanchette married John D. Rockerfeller III, Adelaide wed a successful New England novelist called John Philips Marquand. Helen had partnered Helen Wills Moody, the world champion tennis player, in a doubles tournament. She herself was rated tenth in the tables. Widely read and accomplished, with a disarming personality, she was a sculptor in her own right. This daughter would become the wife of Ernie O'Malley.

That was June 1933. Soon after Ernie went to Chicago and was three months there without a job. How did he live? 'Lilies exist, and so do I,' he said. His first employment was an unlikely one: on the Irish Free State stand at the World Fair! Dorothy Brett was surprised to hear this but she went in search of the Union Avenue building which housed the display. She finally located it, but Ernie was not to be found. 'Weary and disgusted I cruised round among the cases and suddenly saw among the crowd a familiar figure sitting at a large desk. . . reading solemnly in specs. . . red hair plastered down. . . I went up quietly and tapped on the desk. . . Ernie looked up. . . then jumped up excitedly and gave me such a whacking kiss that the crowd around laughed.' A delighted pair chatted and laughed. Ernie dined with Dorothy's party and took the following day off to meet them at a modern painting exhibition where 'he spent the whole day trundling around.' Dorothy told how Ernie had to meet the Irish officers that evening and attend the horse show with them, how she hoped to find a job for him — and how she felt about the promotion: 'Some of the homespuns were lovely. . . otherwise the Irish show was junk.'

One of the best examples of Ernie O'Malley's impish sense of humour was in connection with a flea-circus at the fair. He told how it had a flea named Pat which waved a green flag with 'his or her or perhaps bisexual hands.' He wrote a letter to the Free State consul, describing himself as the daughter of an old Fenian. In it, he expressed disapproval about the derogatory inference of the flea circus, especially since Pat had been picked up in a Dublin hotel! Ernie claimed to have discovered that a letter of complaint to the World Fair management was ready for despatch when somebody pointed out that the whole thing was obviously a joke. Helen and her sister, Adelaide, visited the Fair. When it ended, some say, Ernie became a taxi-driver for a while — in spite of his driving record! In any event, he considered Chicago 'a city without a centre!'

Before the end of 1933 Prohibition had been repealed and Ernie O'Malley was back in New York. He travelled by a hot, stuffy bus. Greasy from the clammy atmosphere, the other passengers remained dourly silent when he suggested opening a window. He endured the discomfort for a while, but then asked a woman would she mind if he let in some air. She did! Her child might catch cold. An angry Ernie opened it just the same. Later he said, 'Better a baby to die than ten grown-ups.'

He borrowed Theodora Goddard's flat while she was away for Christmas, but the New Year was particularly trying. He wondered often where his next meal would come from or outside which bus station he would sleep. Although he described New York as a mess, he also expressed a certain affection for its way of life. He studied old and middle Irish as well as German and French literature. He delivered unpaid-for lectures at New York University. He wrote a considerable number of articles and short stories then.

In May, he went to the country and slept rough in the woods, living off rabbits and fowl. Then he became a Transient on Federal Relief. There were indications that he was finding it difficult to complete his manuscript — possibly due to his erratic employment situation.

One of his occupations was that of house-painter at Hartford House. A particular painting job caused him great distress for he had to mix the colours in an ill-ventilated basement. This led to nausea and, since he was bent over, painting floors at the time, he often got violently sick. But it earned him a bed, some food and two dollars a week. At another painting assignment he fell off a ladder, crashing through a skylight and becoming hung up on another further below. He suffered a little from shock but there were no physical injuries. He described his situation as Gilbert and Sullivan and Dante's *Inferno* all rolled into one. Yet he completed his manuscript and began submitting it to publishers.

During this period, Ernie met Padraic Colum for the first time. The poet and folklorist did not impress him, especially when he talked about Collins and Griffith until Ernie was 'ready to clap his little green hat down on his head.' He had a feeling that Padraic could have expedited a more rapid reading of his manuscript by one particular publisher. The notorious delaying tactics of publishers annoyed Ernie. While he praised some who wrote encouraging letters, he condemned those who acclaimed his work but would not follow up with an acceptance. His work had been with nine houses and he was beginning to despair. He turned to writing short stories but admitted they were not good. He did have six poems published in *Poetry,* and he spent some time compiling anthologies of Irish, British and American poetry. He also began to realise that introductions to the right people were important.

One of his best friends about this time was Rebecca Civcovitz, an artistic lady from Van Cartland Park, whose brother Israel taught at the Julliard School of Music. He admired the way their mother and father were so kind and understanding of their offsprings' talents and their creative inclinations.

There developed a situation whereby Ernie sought work in such places as the big A&P superstores or as 'bus boy' in a restaurant, while enjoying *La Dolce Vita* by night. He attended lectures, plays and art exhibitions and was closely associated with the Group Theatre. He lectured on Irish history and culture to Irish-American organisations.

In May 1935, Ernie was recovering from pneumonia when he decided on returning to Ireland. Under the 1934

Pension Act he was entitled to a general's pension. Also, he hoped to remain a few years during which time he would re-write his manuscript. He had some fears about being obstructed in his homecoming by 'officers of the Ministry' — on which side of the Atlantic was unclear! His visa had expired but his brother, Desmond, then in the merchant navy, smuggled him out. Soon he was home in Iona Drive, Glasnevin.

Meanwhile, Helen Huntington Hooker, her sister, Adelaide and their mother went to Japan with the Garden Club of America. The two girls continued through China, Manchuria to Moscow and on to London. Adelaide met her future husband on the trip and Helen arrived in Dublin in August to plan her wedding. This took place on 27 September, in London. Ernie's two brothers and two sisters attended. After a short honeymoon, the couple returned to Dublin to live at 229 Upper Rathmines Road.

Ernie re-commenced his medical studies once again but he spent most of his time in the library. Peadar O'Donnell heard that Ernie was thinking of destroying his manuscript. He laid hands on it and carried out some judicious editing. There soon followed a memorandum of agreement from Rich and Cowan of 25 Soho Square, London. *On Another Man's Wound* was to be published at eight shillings and six pence for the ordinary edition and two guineas for the limited edition of 51 copies. On that edition, Ernie was to receive a 25% royalty; 15% on ordinary sales up to 5,000 copies; 20% thereafter.

What a great day it must have been for Ernie O'Malley when his work was finally published. Six pages of his manuscript, describing the torture he received after his Inistiogue capture, were omitted. They were subsequently included in the 1961 Four Square edition. On the first copy of the book, Ernie wrote, 'This book is for myself and my heart's curse on whoever takes it.'

Seán Ó Faolain reviewed it in the October 1936 edition of *Ireland Today*. He began:

> The Hero, having lived with the intensity of natural un-consciousness, here turns, with the enlarged personality

of maturity, with nerves and mind made tranquil by time, to the task of conveying the effect of what once was fact. Thus deliberating on what was once undeliberated upon his success depended largely on integrity — on remembering no more than experience, of conveying no more than was felt; art could, and must, be added, but life must be respected. O'Malley has accomplished the difficult task finely. He has achieved his aim. He has given us a book as heroic as *Revolt in the Desert*. Had he but struck to his ends more arrow-like, curbed his lip for writing as much as he did for fighting, it need not have been inferior as literature; and, as it stands, it lacks but one or two things — chiefly nakedness, and after that pity. Also, there is no irony, and in our times the epic note seems to require something like irony — the antidote to romantic over-seriousness.

The reviewer remarked on the book's well-sustained Irish formula of tension and contrasts evoked by death and loneliness, so hard and so tender, but he felt certain people would be inclined to murmur 'Hemingway'. Ó Faoláin's next observation was particularly valid, however:

> As to the absence of pity — it may be thought that this is, in the main, a soldier's record and that there was then little room for that unmasculine (but not unmanly) emotion. This is where, I feel, O'Malley has made the mistake of keeping too precisely to the emotions of the time he describes; there must be many things that were at the time only dimly perceived — thrust away under pressure — that steal now to the surface of memory with greater import than he allowed them at the time. For instance, there is a fine chapter (Chapter X) commenting at large on the country-folk. It must give any foreign friend a graphic picture of what we are like; but is it not too abstract, too pragmatic, too cold and would it not have been enriched with more tenderness, more advertence to the elemental, frail, lyrical qualities of life in the fields? There is another writer who also rebuffs these idle, secret, womanish tendrils of life — Peadar O'Donnell, and I am wondering if the reason is not the same;

that both are bitten by the sociological bug that both want, only, the virtues that *work*.

(Peadar O'Donnell has stated that Ernie was not a man of social ideas but would come down on the right side when the facts were put before him.) Seán's critique continued:

> 1 think we are entitled to say these things about this book: that it would have been better, fine as it is, had it been more simple and more soft. In a sense this kind of book is a collaboration: it is not quite the same thing as a literary man's job of work, or an artist's book; it tends to become the property of the nation and the nation will, as it does, hail it as the idealisation of the guerrilla, long awaited, worth waiting for since it comes finely at last; in a sense the nation dictated it, and it will rest on our shelves, beside Tone and Mitchel as the expression of a period. . . no critic but must say of it that it has added another name to the permanent list of Irish men of letters.

Ó Faolain had wondered about O'Malley's memory. He opined that no guerrilla fighter wandering about the countryside during all seasons could resist the temptation to evoke 'that immense sense of nature feeding into the tired heart'. But he feared that the 'natural background' might have been propounded in O'Malley's studio. What read well was not *remembered,* he felt, so he wondered was it *seen* at all. The February crocus, the March daffodil, the April primrose and the June iris all bloomed in O'Malley's spring. The critic was precise but the Irish spring has always been flexible to the storyteller and these flowers have ever been linked with the first season, however inaccurately.

More than the nation hailed the work. *The Times* (London) said O'Malley was a man of high artistic and literary quality. *The New Republic* described the book as 'swift and exciting'.

When the book appeared in the United States a year later under the title *Army Without Banners,* Ernie O'Malley's work won considerable acclaim. The *New York Herald Tribune's* reviewer Maurice Joy described it as:

A stirring tale of heroic adventure. . . told without Rancour or Rhetoric. . . not only superbly written [but] a book of revaluation. . .

I do not know of any other [work] which better enables one to understand how it came about that the decrepit and morbid Irish nationalism of a generation ago was replaced by that flaming spirit which has achieved the substance, if not yet the outward shape of political sovereignty. Happily, the revelation is kept incidental to the truly heroic narrative. Mr O'Malley, a deft and scrupulous craftsman, has told the story for the story's sake.

The story, of course, was worth telling to Americans. O'Malley had spent a considerable time there so both himself and the struggle he narrated fired the imagination of that freedom-loving nation. Mr Joy continued his complimentary appraisal with expressions like: 'The spirit of his writing is detached from polemics of any sort', and 'His epic and idyllic qualities blend easily as he pauses in the middle of a fighting record to tell of the plaintive cry of a bird or its curious flight under a low, gray sky over a country haunted by preternatural memories.'

R. L. Duffus was the reviewer for the *New York Times*. He was enthusiastic in his praise for the work under its American title. First he tells of O'Malley being 'brought up in a "shoneen town" — that is, one where people aped John Bull until they themselves were "little John Bulls".' Then he applauded the author for giving us lightning flashes rather than connected narrative — the things that are remembered rather than the things that the narrator has bothered to look up.'

So R. L. Duffus praised what others condemned — not unusual in book-reviewing. (A *Kerryman* correspondent, Francis Andrews, also forgave O'Malley for 'the occasional errors that must inevitably occur when writing years afterwards of specific incidents'). *The New York Times* continued:

What will haunt the reader longest is not altogether the escapes, the fighting. . . not these stirring, dreadful and romantic elements, but the picture of a country and a people seen through danger. Danger may be a depressant which alters the flow of the internal secretions and produces various kinds of madness, from abject fear to utter recklessness, but in Mr O'Malley it produced clarity and intensity of sight. It brought out the poet in him — and also the mystic, as when he went by night to the schoolhouse of Strokestown, under the ridge of Slievebawn, to summon the legendary Black Pig to come forth.

How delighted must the *New York Times* readers have been at the reviewer's description of the pig as given by O'Malley in as splendid a fashion as any Dowra *seanachaidhe* and of the unaccepted challenge when 'no ridge of spines or yellow eyes came out.' The author's simple pungent style received praise but there were some slight reservations too:

Mr O'Malley will tell us little of his subjective sensations. He does not let us know how he felt when he first fired to kill. He does, however, make us see, hear, almost smell what happened.

As he unfolded how 'little by little the sentiment of the country solidified behind the revolutionists', the reviewer accorded his final accolade:

The story. . . will probably do the English good. They should be glad, at least, that they did not succeed in shooting or hanging Ernie O'Malley, and so killing before it was born a stirring and beautiful book.

People like Seán O'Casey and Robert Kee have also praised the work. The remark of M. J. MacManus of the *Irish Press* rings clearer than most when he describes *On Another Man's Wound* as 'a narrative that is stamped from the first page to the last with the rich, many-sided personality of its author.'

The book was an instant success, but the joy following this was shortlived. A libel action was taken against the author. Early in 1937, Ernie lost the libel case.

Later in 1938 the story appeared in a German translation: *Rebelien in Irland* Erlebniße eines Irischen Freiheitskampfers, übersetzt von Karl Breuer, Berlin: Metzner. (*Rebellion in Ireland*, Adventures of an Irish Freedom Fighter, translated by Karl Breuer, Berlin: Metzner.)

Ernie wondered about touring the continent? Or would he bring young Eithne Golden over to Ireland to help him collect and collate folklore and traditional music and song? What about the Spanish Civil War? It had become an ideological struggle for European states. Communist and left wing sympathisers from many countries, including Ireland, swelled the ranks of the International Brigades of the republican forces there.

In his book *Connolly Column,* Michael O'Riordan stated that Ernie O'Malley was associated with Peadar O'Donnell in the task of defending Republican Spain. This was not so. Peadar O'Donnell recalled Ernie speaking spiritedly on behalf of Republican Spain at the Engineer's Hall, Dawson Street. 'In any concrete struggle he'd be sure to come down on the side of the oppressed. He understood Fascism and was ideologically opposed to it. But he had no illusions about the war — a conspiracy of the landed aristocracy was at the basis of it.'

Ernie finally abandoned his medical studies. On a trip to Paris he met Samuel Beckett, and bought paintings by Vlaminck, Lurcat and Marchand. He and Helen occupied a new flat at Fitzwilliam Place and used it as a base for research, photographic expeditions, etc., in which they were both interested. Ernie was fascinated by early Irish Christian art and he wished to show Helen more of Ireland. So they set about making a photographic record of the country's old monasteries and ecclesiastical buildings.

Like many before them, the O'Malleys were captivated by the west of Ireland and felt an urge to settle there. Evidence of a period spent at Old Head Lodge, Kilsallagh, is slight. There is little doubt, however, but that Helen was intrigued by the story of the great O'Malley clan, by the vibrant lore of Clew Bay and its Burke strongholds and the great western queen Grace O'Malley who married Richard Burke and who accumulated fortresses all along the coast. Did not she downface Queen Elizabeth I — and in the regal lady's own palace too! *Granuaile ag teacht thár saile!*

They travelled to Burrishoole one sunny day in 1938. Ernie's sister Kaye was minding the baby in the car. As they crossed the picturesque Burrishoole Bridge an old man leaned on the wall. They saw a resemblance to Luke Malley in the face. 'I'll bet his name is O'Malley,' said Ernie. It was, but no relation. 'Throw a stone in Mayo and you'll strike an O'Malley,' they say.

Nearby was Burrishoole Lodge. Ernie and Helen loved it, so they rented it for a period and later bought it. It stood between Carraig an Chabhlaigh, where Granuaile lived, and Burrishoole Abbey, one of the places said to hold her remains. (Clare Island is a more likely spot.)

They moved in and Helen combined her artistic flair with her love of things Irish in her interior design. There were tweed curtains homespun in the Mayo mountains; indeed, a guest room may have been completely designed and furnished from the county. Works of art filled the place. Here was tasteful living among ancient and historic surroundings.

At one stage Ernie injured his right hand and it did not set well. He continued to row in Clew Bay — against medical advice. More endurance testing? Innocent of opinions held about his driving, he naïvely proclaimed that he had learned to drive perfectly with his left hand. He finally wrote inviting Eithne Golden over for the history-folklore-music collection. He hoped she would learn the technique and go back home and collect the vast store available in the United States. He offered her the fare and a contact in the consulate to help her arrangements — surely not the recipient of his 'Pat the Flea' complaint! Eithne did not come.

Ernie's sister Kaye remembered an incident when a meal of lamb and mint sauce had been prepared. A bottle of wine was placed on the table. Ernie's fastidiousness made itself apparent when he made to give the meat to the dog, proclaiming the impropriety of serving wine with vinegar. Kaye protested, saying she wanted her meal no matter what culinary sacrilege had been committed. Ernie stamped outside to work off his anger — perhaps by a little ploughing which he sometimes attempted. An O'Malley relative once claimed that he was 'impossible to live with'.

His strength ebbed and surged. Winters he found hard, Ireland too. 'A hard, cruel and bitter country,' he declared, 'but with faults counterbalanced by kindness, humanity and faith; warped by an abundance of failure, but attempting everything still. It was best seen with clay on the boots and salt water on the hands,' he ventured. It could be sighted intellectually in the city — but around too many drawing-room fires. Yet he longed for his Dublin home, where he would not be forced to fashion his own intellectual life and make it self-supporting. There were no libraries 'worth a small curse', no art or artists within miles of Burrishoole — few people who read, even. He still wrote plenty of literary criticism. Of Frank O'Connor's book on Michael Collins, *The Big Fellow,* he said that it was a peculiar medley of information and misinformation. 'He wants to create a realistic legend or rather to brick up a legend.'

There have been suggestions that Ernie O'Malley joined Tom Barry, Liam Deasy and others in the Military College with a view to accepting a commission in the army after the outbreak of the Second World War. In view of the fact that he was in receipt of a temporary disability pension, this seems unlikely; yet he said in a letter dated 4 July 1940 that he had joined up, 'but they haven't taken me so far'. The apparent paradox may possibly be explained by the fact that he did move around Southern Command Local Defence Force Area in a type of advisory role. He felt that the regular army wished to run things its own way and did not wish to be bothered with 'us ex-soldiers'. He expressed no bitterness; just the opinion that their services would be welcomed, come the invasion. He appeared to be convinced that the country would be invaded by the Germans or the British or both simultaneously. He worked hard making Burrishoole into a model farm, adding many innovations. Yet he sadly expressed his appreciation of having 'these last few years here' and opined that the Irish had never been safe and were always content to die — in groups if not as individuals.

A Dublin home was maintained at 15 Whitebeam Avenue, Clonskeagh, and it was while there that Ernie showed how he was still capable of a flash of cavalier behaviour. A story is told of how he objected to a certain expression of opinion voiced in a newspaper about his War of Independence involvement. He called to the home of Andy McDonnell and asked him if he had a few hours to spare; that he wanted him along as he was going to shoot the correspondent. Younger and more tolerant of opinion, Andy was also aware of Ernie's temper. He was quite serious about the intended killing, Andy thought.

Winking at his wife, he said, 'All right, Ernie, but I want to call to Tony Woods on the way.' They left, and Andy's wife, responding to her husband's nod, rang Tony Woods and told him what was happening. Tony planned how to take the heat out of the situation. When the pair called he commenced an argument with Ernie about a particular execution that had taken place during the Civil War. Ernie rose to the bait and became so involved in the debate that he forgot completely about his planned assassination.

The Dublin home was often visited by people of the theatre and the art world. In fact, in spite of the keen interest in the theatre he had shown at university and the theatre's programmes which appeared among his memorabilia, Ernie once complained that his wife over-ran the place with members of an amateur dramatic company.

In 1945 Ernie was again ill when Florrie O'Donoghue wrote to him concerning a proposal for a systematic collection of all the records of actions against the Black and Tans. The fine historian Lieutenant General M. J. Costello was mentioned as an invaluable source. Ernie was researching a series of radio talks about the North Cork and other Brigade actions which were eventually transmitted in 1953.

In January of that year he reviewed Thomas Mac-Greevy's *Jack B. Yeats, An Appreciation and an Interpretation*. The critique appeared in *The Bell*, then under Seán Ó Faolain's editorship. Ernie felt it strange that this was the first work to be published on the paintings of Yeats, an artist who brought 'a fresh vision and a creative palette' to Irish landscapes. He declared that there was no national painting tradition and that the English colonial tradition of academic painting was 'more hidebound than its mother tradition'; yet this was the standard by which works of art were assessed here. (He was close to Yeats and had worked hard assisting Jack's 1945 National Exhibition.)

In June of that year, this time under Peadar O'Donnell's editorial hand, *The Bell*'s feature article was contributed by Earnán Ó Máille. 'The School of London' offered comment on an exhibition of drawings, paintings and sculpture at the Waddington Gallery which was 'the first comprehensive showing in Dublin of contemporary English work'. Ernie praised the new gallery as being a credit to the architect Robinson and to Victor Waddington's judgement. He rejoiced in the fact that the 'neglected Cinderella, sculpture, had at last been given a good light in which to show its three dimensions.'

In Burrishoole he had visits from people involved in literature and the arts: Nora McGuinness, painter; Bryan MacMahon, author and playwright; Delia Murphy, balladeer. His days teaching the Golden children in Taos stood him in good stead when his own children Cahal, Etain and Cormac became ill and he instructed them himself. He again encouraged with traditional Irish music, sea shanties, early church music. He had four volumes of Haydn, twelve of Mozart, twenty-two of Beethoven, five of Brahms, Chopin, Bach, Sibelius, Wagner, Schubert — the collection was impressive. He wrote playlets for the children to perform. He read to them too. *Moby Dick* was a favourite. 'There is a sense of eternity in each chapter,' Ernie said of it.

Peadar O'Donnell announced in April 1947 that *The Bell*'s former editor Seán Ó Faolain, who had recently been responsible for re-organising the *People and Books* feature, could no longer continue as book editor. Ernie O'Malley took on the task in May and continued to do so for some time.

In 1947, Ernie O'Malley was elected secretary of that distinguished body founded by W. B. Yeats and George Bernard Shaw, the Irish Academy of Letters. On Sunday 7 September in that year the BBC Home Service transmitted programme No. 140 in its *Country Magazine* series. This had been pre-recorded in Dublin during August and it featured Seamus Ennis on tin whistle, Tom Maxwell, Michael Cronin, Albert Healy and Bryan MacMahon among others. Earnán O'Malley was compère. Cormac and Etain flew to the United States and were joined later by Cahal. Ernie went to Achill and Helen to London. Back in Burrishoole in the fall, Ernie expressed concern at having to interrupt Etain's schooling. She had been attending a day school in Killiney while they were in Dublin. Her tonsils were due for removal too, he feared, for she was displaying signs of slight deafness. Worry was also apparent in a letter telling of the boys' recent illness. Cormac was not looking too well, he thought. To cheer things up Ernie began speaking in what he described as an 'Abbey brogue'. The children latched on to this and made incessant demands for another play to be written for them.

Helen visited the United States in October. When Cahal returned from the USA, he went to Glenstal College in Limerick. Ernie wrote on Mexican art in *The Bell*. Helen returned in May 1948 and planned the purchase of a London home. Ernie set out to record interviews with veterans of the War of Independence and Civil War.

The couple were together in June when tuberculosis was suspected in the boys. A further tragedy occurred when Marion, Ernie's sister, was killed in an air crash in France. She had never liked flying but her one-armed husband, who piloted a light plane, was a fanatic. Ernie attended the re-interment of William Butler Yeats' remains in Drumcliff, Sligo. A letter of thanks from Ernie to a friend who assisted in his Civil War research included a significant remark: (Thanks for being so kind) 'about my own particular Civil War.' Helen left finally in August and Ernie began corresponding with Sotheby of London about the sale of his personal library to raise funds.

Friends of the O'Malleys speak with incredulous partisanship about one or the other being to blame for the marriage breakup. Private matters of that kind are better unspoken of. Judgement can only be perfunctory.

Ernie's cousin, Sir John Gilbert Laithwaite, G.C.M.G., K.C.B., K.C.I.E. was appointed United Kingdom representative to the Republic of Ireland in 1949. (He became ambassador in 1950.) By contrast, Ernie O'Malley was then arranging to send Cahal and Etain to the Irish-speaking college at Ring, Co Waterford.

Ernie stayed betimes with Tony Woods at Sandymount. He visited the O'Rahillys too. Some attempts at reconciliation were made by third parties who believed that Helen wanted her 'rebel general' back. In April 1950 Helen took Cahal and Etain to the United States. Divorce proceedings were initiated. In March 1951 she sought an injunction restraining Ernie from remaining in Burrishoole. The constitution was quoted by counsel, on the grounds that it was an attempt to break up the matrimonial home.

Evidence at the trial described Ernie barricading off part of the house, and the drive to the house being lined with men. After consultation between counsel, who later saw the judge in his chambers, the President of the High Court adjourned generally the action seeking possession.

An Interlocutory Decree was entered in El Paso, State of Colorado, on 6 November 1951. Divorce was granted on 6 May 1952. Helen was given custody of Cahal and Etain. Cormac went to Willow Park, Blackrock College and Ernie gave strict instructions about his being allowed only one visitor.

He never let his son out of his strict control during school holidays; driving him around in an old Ford Anglia; visiting Aran; rearing him with the fond wish that he would grow up to do good for the country he loved. An amusing piece of gossip told how he placed barbed wire around Burrishoole and mobilised the former North Mayo IRA battalion to protect his son. Perhaps this story emanated from the evidence given at the trial in March.

On 12 March 1953, Ernie O'Malley collapsed in Dublin. Since October 1945 his temporary disability award had been made a 100% pension. Therefore, after that year he was not eligible for free hospitalisation, but he was admitted to the army's St Bricin's Hospital as a paying patient — some say on the express instruction of the Taoiseach Eamon de Valera. Again rumour proliferated, more so when Ernie was discharged on 27 July. All sorts of people were incorrectly credited with paying his hospital bill.

By the summer of 1954 Ernie had finally moved to a flat in Mespil Road, Dublin. He visited Tony Woods, Christy Smith, Robert Barton in Glendalough and his old friend Johnny Raleigh of Limerick. Johnny owned the large Kilbane House at Castletroy. It contained a guest room where Eamon de Valera frequently slept. Ernie, as of old, would arrive unannounced, stay a while and would then disappear. The family loved to see him come for he filled the household with lively story-telling, anecdote and conversation. A happy period was spent on Aran with Cormac during the summer of 1955.

Newspaper cuttings on a wide range of subjects accumulated alongside music, art and theatre catalogues in Ernie's Dublin flat. His memoirs about his Civil War activities were mounting — but the War of Independence was not yet forgotten. On the sixth anniversary of its first publication, 4 September 1955, the *Sunday Press* began a gigantic series contributed by Ernie O'Malley (published in book form, *Raids and Rallies,* in 1983). 'The Sack of Hollyford' was the first action featured and it took up a complete page. Then followed Drangan, Rineen, Tourmakeady, Scramogue, Rearcross, Carrowkennedy, Knocklong — names which still evoked passions among a people taking their first nose-dive into industrialisation.

Even on Christmas Day the series continued. And what a reaction! Ballads about the various ambushes were sent to the editor in whose letters column the author was taken to task or supported according to the affiliations of the correspondents. Right through the spring and into the summer the series continued, ending on 6 May 1956.

On that day too, the paper carried a photograph of Ernie in Tom Hennigan's column. Lord Killanin and John Ford stood alongside him. This was in connection with a film, *Three Leaves of a Shamrock,* made by the Four Provinces Film Company. It was one of the first films shot entirely on location and it was in three parts — so designed for showing as a full length feature film or as three supports, *The Minute's Wait, The Majesty of the Law* and *The Rising of the Moon.* The last named was shot at Lough Cutra Castle in Galway and it concerned the execution of a prisoner. In the *Sunday Press* picture caption Ernie was described as 'technical adviser', but Lord Killanin remembered his being there also as a friend of John Ford.

Then Ernie was off to Cambridge, England, and the home of Lord Walston in Newton where he had often visited before. Henry David Walston, who ran for Labour in Cambridge in 1951 and 1955, wrote *No More Bread* and *Life on the Land.* His wife Catherine Crompton, previously of Rye, New York, had a grandmother, Sarah McDonald Sheridan, who was a friend of the Hooker family and acted as companion to the Hooker girls at one time. It was through Helen that both couples met and became friendly. Ernie became ill while there.

Over the Christmas period Ernie's family in Dublin met at Kevin's home in Merrion Square where he had a successful practice. It was decided that Ernie should not die in England. But what to do? Kathleen's (Kaye) husband Captain Harry Hogan offered to take him. He was then a serving officer and Kaye was in the army nursing service. Kevin went over to England and found that Ernie's heart condition had greatly deteriorated. He arranged for his return to Ireland and for his admission to the Mater Hospital.

All his prickliness seemed to have disappeared when Kaye and Harry were eventually allowed to take him to their home at Nashville Park, Howth, at the end of January. He saw a certain humour in the situation. One evening when Kaye was attending to his sore back, Harry was present in the room. Ernie had to be turned. With a glint of devilment in his eye he grinned and said, as Harry came to help: 'Bloody good enough for a Free Stater to roll me over and rub my bottom; let him do it, Kathleen!'

He had almost forgotten the divisions at that stage. Lack of interest had replaced bitterness. He felt that the good which the old warriors had set out to help achieve had gone by the wayside along which now trundled a bandwagon laden with fat wagoneers.

Ernie O'Malley, fighter, writer, character extraordinary, departed this life on 25 March 1957. Obituaries were generous in their praise.

'A man of high artistic and literary quality, as well as a daring fighter,' said the *Irish Times*.

'A proud tribute to a brave man,' said the *Irish Press;* and it continued, saying that, 'throughout his relatively short life [he] symbolised the ideals which led to the freedom of the greater part of Ireland.'

Ernie O'Malley's remains were removed to the Church of the Assumption, Howth, where his tricolour-draped coffin was borne by surviving members of the Four Courts garrison. Helen and her husband Richard, and Ernie's children Cahal, Etain and Cormac attended the funeral on 27 March. Ernie's mother, Marion, his sister Kathleen and brothers, Surgeon Cecil, Dr Kevin, Dr Brendan and Paddy were present. Mass was celebrated by Very Rev. Patrick O'Keeffe P.P. The President and Mrs Seán T. Ó Ceallaigh were there with the Taoiseach, Eamon de Valera, members of the judiciary, the Oireachtas and the defence forces. The Army No. 1 Band led the cortège from the church.

Young people lined the footpaths with their elders, eager to be part of this tribute to a colourful, daring and learned soldier and academic. The interment itself was highly appropriate for Ernie O'Malley. There were sharp orders in Irish from an army officer of a new generation. (He would have liked the military precision.) The triple volley cracked its staccato salute. (Ceremonial appealed to him.)

Then the swelling and dying notes of the Last Post and Reveille rang out, mournful first, then sprightly across Tolka's valley. (City and country, both ever appealing to him.) Seán Moylan delivered an oration:

> He becomes in his death part of Ireland's tradition, and a nation must have roots. The memory of the efforts and courage of Ernie O'Malley will be preserved in the hearts of those who have a pride in and an appreciation of the high moral value of national freedom, otherwise we cannot hope to preserve and develop those qualities essential to the realisation of our hopes for our country. . . *Toisc go raibh a leithéid ann beidh a leithéid arís ann. Ní ghá dúinn eagla ar son an náisiúin, ní baol dí de bhrí an sompla d' fag sé dúinn.*

Dan Breen wept and a Christian Brother who had taught Ernie O'Malley remembered a phrase from a poem: 'tears of warlike men'.

O'Malley's book on the Civil War, entitled *The Singing Flame,* was published by Anvil Books in 1978. The manuscript which Ernie himself had prepared was edited by Frances-Mary Blake.

# 6

# Soldier, Man and Patron
# of the Arts

*Our flag upon the battlements*
*Is to the breeze out-thrown*
*And with God's grace we'll keep it there*
*In spite of Queen and throne.*
*There's many a brave O'Malley here*
*With me to man the walls*
*And rally round the flag we love*
*Until the last man falls!*

*O'Malley — The Soldier*

In *Survivors,* Tony Lyons, IRA staff captain is quoted as saying that Ernie O'Malley was only a third-rate general, a great man in many ways but not to be compared with Liam Pilkington, Tom Barry or Tom Maguire.

Todd Andrews, in *Dublin Made Me,* said:

> O'Malley had taken part in more attacks on British soldiers, Black and Tans and RIC than any other IRA man in Ireland. He had been wounded many times. Once he was captured and tortured by the Auxiliaries in Kilkenny and taken to Dublin to be court-martialled for murder but he made a sensational escape. He was 'le plus brave des braves'. While he was generally admired he was not generally liked. He had the reputation of being a martinet, of being intolerant of anyone who did not come up to his almost impossibly high standards of valour or endurance. But worse, he was thought to be an intellectual. When men were gossiping around the

fireside he held himself aloof reading, it was said, *Epictetus* or *The Vedas*. In my association with him I had no complaint against him on this score. I never knew of him reading a book nor did he embarrass me by discussing them. To the contrary, I was surprised at a certain element of frivolity he displayed.

The student of O'Malley's adult life finds himself constantly groping to defend the man against unkind judgements. As Dr Andrews suggests, reading and intellectual pursuits are not popular in the gregarious cameraderie enjoyed by soldiers.

O'Malley's military role further alienated him. The 'man from GHQ' was likely to be regarded with not a little suspicion, as someone who did not know the real facts and who was trying to ram the opinions of officialdom down the necks of men in the field, men who daily had to contend with problems in their own way. This would have been particularly true of country units. Here was a man bedecked in uniform or a bread coloured trench-coat with guns, map-cases and binoculars hanging from his person; aloof, harsh, 'gildy' and running things 'by the book'.

His conversations, when he indulged, were more likely to have praised certain great masters rather than Master McGrath, accomplished painters rather than fine hurlers. He was a man who 'said poems' rather than 'rendered recitations'.

Ernie O'Malley himself was concerned about this. He studied the profession of arms — this is apparent from manuals and books of instruction of his held by Sighle Humphreys — but he found that in putting his knowledge into practice he drove too much and did not lead sufficiently. He worried too that his judgement of men may have been influenced by what he lacked in Gaelic outlook and traditions. Ernie O'Malley's background may have given him many unhappy moments as he attempted to apply military methods to a parish militia situation.

Seán MacBride had 'tremendous respect and admiration for O'Malley'. Peadar O'Donnell felt he would have made a better chief-of-staff than Liam Lynch. Piaras Béaslaí stated that Michael Collins had a high opinion of Ernie as a fighting man.

Ernie O'Malley admitted to knowing fear — even terror. Such an admission is in itself commendable. It also makes his deeds of bravery even more laudable, for it is in the conquest of fear that courage reaches towards greatness. Even the most vehement critics of O'Malley admit to his gallantry.

In *The Singing Flame,* Ernie alluded to 'momentary pleasure that I had in hitting a mark'. This would suggest a certain killer instinct in the man, a paradox when there is evidence that he was loath to fire first (see pages 21 and 25).

In Bill Hammond's book *Soldier of the Rearguard,* Matt Flood of Cork No. 2 Brigade described O'Malley as a great soldier, fighter and leader who would adopt a prone position on a high bank during an ambush, although he kept his men under cover. He described Ernie's fine fieldcraft as he trained others to move in bounds, judging the time taken by an enemy to manipulate a rifle-bolt. Matt, who had British army experience, told an anecdote of O'Malley arriving one day as he was instructing in the Hotchkiss machine-gun. Ernie insisted on sitting down behind the weapon despite being warned that it was loaded. A woman milking a cow nearby soon ran for her life as bullets riddled her milk bucket and left milk spurting through a number of holes. Undismayed, O'Malley said everything was all right and carried on as if nothing had happened.

Ernie O'Malley's opinion of other soldiers was sometimes harsh. While owning that Kevin O'Higgins had talents for the classics and literature, he found him 'incorrigibly addicted to practical joking'.* He did not trust Dick Mulcahy. He criticised Liam Lynch for not issuing explicit orders. However, he regarded Cathal Brugha as 'the most uncompromising of all the army officers'. Kathleen Napoli McKenna regarded Ernie as the uncompromising personification of the struggle for the Republic. She described him as 'fanatical'. 'It was impossible,' she said, 'to doubt his

* O'Malley Papers, University College Dublin Archives.

THE ERNIE O'MALLEY STORY

sincerity, not to admire his courage, his uncompromising Republican stand.'

When Francis Stuart reviewed *The Singing Flame* in the *Sunday Press* he told how, in the early spring of 1945, he himself was trudging along behind the advancing French troops at Lake Constance which straddles the Swiss-German border. German soldiers stopped him and, seeing his Irish passport, a lieutenant enquired of him if he knew Ernie O'Malley. He had read his first book and was impressed by Ernie's story.

Michael McInerney said he was callous in his *Singing Flame* description of Paddy O'Brien picking off a sniper firing on the Four Courts. On reading the passage, the charge seems unfounded. Michael also commented that, 'like many Republicans, O'Malley had little sense of social problems, though radical militarily, and apparently he was almost unaware of the North. . . Like Pearse, his great hero was Cuchulain. But the Cuchulains don't hold the solution. But then, O'Malley didn't live long enough to write his own conclusion.' Michael said he emerged from the book as '"the unrepentant Fenian", perhaps even as the very first Provisional, intransigent, intractable and uncompromising in his attitude to all authority, even military authority.'

To Liam O'Flaherty, Ernie was 'a good friend' whose patriotism and leadership as a general in the 1920s was greatly admired.

An unbiased study of Ernie O'Malley's military career suggests that he was a man of outstanding courage who strove to be professional in his approach to guerrilla warfare, which can dehumanise and bring out savage traits in a man. This very aspiration made him unpopular among his colleagues. Such is often the price which a dedicated soldier has to pay.

## O'Malley — The Man

Tony Woods, another IRA staff captain greatly respected by his contemporaries, described Ernie O'Malley as 'a very flamboyant and extrovert character'. Sighle Humphreys, on the other hand, regarded him as reticent. Marion O'Rahilly agreed with that assessment, adding that his apparent harshness and brusqueness were attempts to cover up an innate shyness.

He has been described as complex, self-centred, eccentric, interesting and prickly. 'He took people for granted.' 'He had ambitions about being an arts' connoisseur.' 'He had a marvellous sense of humour — if you could get at it.' 'He was cantankerous — but it was because of his dreadful wounds.' 'He had a good sense of fun — of an intellectual content.' 'He was difficult to live with and took it for granted that people should administer to him.' 'He had a lively mind. Curiosity of life caused his wanderings.' 'He was hard on himself.' 'He was very willing to endure fatigue.' 'He imposed on his friends.'

Bryan MacMahon visited Ernie in Burrishoole Lodge and O'Malley visited him while in Listowel for the races. Bryan found him quiet, reserved and restrained. He had a clear-cut, straight mind moving from A to B. He was not very loquacious, 'but he was wonderful — a man of legends.'* Bryan wrote of the 'revolutionary *par excellence*', redheaded and with chiselled features', who had prints of rifle-butts on his face 'where he was battered as a prisoner in Dublin Castle'. A man who refused to compromise, he was 'ruthless for the right, scholarly, ingenuous in certain ways.'

David Neligan, an agent for Michael Collins in Dublin Castle, regarded Ernie as having been a remarkable man. As his enemy in the Civil War, he recognised him as a thoroughly dangerous man, 'which implies daring, organising talents and dedication to his cause.' He also described him as 'chivalrous in a war not noted for its chivalry.'

Interviews with O'Malley's contemporaries all tend to

* *Here's Ireland*, B. T. Batsford Ltd, London 1971.

leave the impression that because of his courageous qualities, his daring and enthusiasm for the fight, his colleagues were reluctant to criticise unduly. Some scolded gently:

'He was a charmer with a detachable manner, depending on the company.'

'He had a sense of boisterous fun but not a sense of humour.'

'He pretended intellectual qualities which he hadn't got.'

This statement must be challenged. Irishmen are in the habit of deriding persons who appear to possess an artistic temperament. This sometimes comes about through a peculiar jealousy which makes itself manifest when two people who engage in intellectual pursuits come in contact. It is something close to fear of being outdone in appreciation of the arts. It may also arise because of a society which declares that to become a man, a youth must be a hurler or footballer, must drink porter and perhaps use foul language. A sensitive, aesthetic interest is 'sissyish'; a devotee of literature or the arts is 'peculiar'; a recluse is 'half f——ing mad'.

Ernie O'Malley was reared in an 'establishment' house where he felt the power of the empire. In the hills and the bogs he realised a different power — the resilience of the people. So he emerged as a complex character. He displayed little early interest in the Irish language but he did develop a regard for the Gaelic tradition. He frequently used the Irish form of his name, Earnán Ó Máille and he affixed an 'O' to his registered English name Malley.

There are very few photographs of Ernie O'Malley. In *On Another Man's Wound,* he told how he disliked the taking of his first photograph because he had been told to look at the birdy and there had been none. He also described the rounds taken to avoid being photographed after his Inistiogue arrest by the British. Mrs Eithne Golden Sax of New York owns a picture of him in what she described as a 'typical pose' — thoughtful and contemplative — at Acoa Pueblo. The National Library holds a fine picture of him in his later years and a drawing by Seán O'Sullivan hangs in the National Gallery. The most interesting picture is from

an un-named newspaper and shows a handsome mous-
tached young man in uniform, holding a Mauser. The
caption reads:

> This interesting and unique photograph was taken
> under somewhat peculiar circumstances during the
> Anglo-Irish War. What a number of the 'boys' down
> south really wanted photographed was the 'Peter the
> Painter'. Shy, though brave, no one could be got to hold
> it. At last Ernie O'Malley (Republican candidate for
> Dublin North) was prevailed upon to do the needful,
> and thus was taken the only photo of him in existence
> (save one taken when he was a baby) which is now in his
> mother's possession.

In an interview with Pierre Joannon, Consul General
d'Irlande at Antibes, Graham Greene said of Ernie, 'He
was an enchanting man. I remember, one day in Achill, I
asked him at what time high tide was. He hesitated a long
time, a look of caution came into his eyes and his attitude
became typical of the Old IRA man determined not to give
any information to a possible enemy. "Well, Graham, that
depends," said he laconically in the end.'

On many occasions in his writings, he commented on
religion. Like many of his colleagues, he resented the
admonishment of their activities by the clergy, particularly
the Bishops' Pastoral of 10 October 1922 (see page 54).

He could also see the funny side of religion. He told a
humorous story of being on the run and sleeping in a safe
house where father and son shared a bed. He overheard the
Litany of Loreto being recited as follows:

> Ark of the Covenant — Pray for us.
> Gate of Heaven — Pray for us.
> Move up in the bed, Patsy.
> Morning Star — Pray for us.
> Patsy, take in your fat arse out of that.
> Help of the sick — Pray for us.
> Refuge of sinners — Pray for us.

When refused the sacraments before his threatened
execution, he sought a copy of the *Imitation of Christ*. This

is a book of meditations and it seems reasonable to surmise that Ernie was a deep thinker about his faith. If speculation were to be carried further, it could be argued that its contents may have had an influence on his life. There are thoughts on disorderly affection, too much familiarity, the advantage of adversity, love of solitude and silence, bearing all that is painful.

Ernie O'Malley had a stoic unconcern for discomfort and a resolute attitude to the endurance of pain. During the wars he almost appeared to like pain; he certainly did little to avoid it and he never allowed it to affect his activities.

Opinions of Ernie O'Malley offered by his contemporaries are remarkable for their contradictions. But the words of William James must always be heeded: whenever two people meet there are really six people present. There is each man as he sees himself, each man as the other person sees and each man as he really is.

### O'Malley — The Patron of the Arts

They strike with the pen and the tongue and the wink
and the nod and the leer —
   The Knockers.
All God-fearing men; Praises sung — 'Have a drink',
'Such a cod' — as they jeer —
   The Knockers.
'Oh flourish, dear Ireland, and fill up our skins;  make
us loved and respected' —
   The Knockers.
'Praise landlord and squire, but bad cess to our kin; let
them be retroflected' —
   The Knockers.*

Nowhere are the nation's 'Knockers' as thick on the ground as in the area of the arts. Let anyone acquire the most elementary knowledge of the creative or performing arts, then lo and behold, he becomes a critic overnight!

* *Life Train*, P. O'Farrell.

Ernie O'Malley's interest in the arts has been cynically observed upon by some of his contemporaries. They point to his corrections and personal comments written on eminent works and condemn him as arrogant — even foolish. They do not allow for the fact that unpublished notes might well be merely formative opinion, perhaps little more than recorded thoughts for future probing and open to later rejection.

For example, on a copy of Vasari's *Lives of Italian Painters,* selected and prefaced by Havelock Ellis, O'Malley wrote on the endpapers. He gave his opinion of Florentine art and compared Massacio, Fra' Angelico and others. Perspective, realism, problems of light and shade, passion for movement, grouping and composition were discussed. Some sentences were poorly constructed and some ridicule was levelled towards Ernie as a result.

A competent assessor, however, offered the view that Ernie's reasonings were astute and reasonable. He was, after all, part of a movement, running wildly through Europe, against classic art in favour of post-impressionism and all forms of individualism. Henri Matisse's stylised designs and Pablo Picasso's cubism were emerging as victors over works of Perugino and Raphael.

In Ireland, Jack B. Yeats was pro-IRA, pro-nationalist and pro the future. He based his work on a love of the land, literature and the private man. Ernie had quite a significant and well chosen collection of Yeats' paintings.

His papers contain articles on Cezanne, Van Gogh, Blake and others as well as reports on art exhibitions all over America as well as Europe and Ireland. They also hold a huge collection of reviews from newspapers and journals, photographs, drawings and all the bric-a-brac of the enthusiast.

He reviewed in *The Bell* as we have seen. James White, art critic from 1940 and Director of the National Gallery from 1964 to 1980, stated that he always respected Ernie O'Malley as a reviewer. His writing on Jack B. Yeats was perceptive and sympathetic and he was part of a circle which included Jack Yeats, Tom McGreevy, Con Curran and Victor Waddington, all of whom respected him.

His position as the author and participant in Ireland's struggles for freedom was a useful weapon in the modern movement in art in Ireland through the 'thirties and the 'forties. People today could hardly imagine the opposition and resistance which had to be overcome in the echelons of establishment and conservatism — particularly in government and clerical areas.

An idea of the range of Ernie O'Malley's interests can be gained from his papers in the UCD archives. Among his copious notes on and about art there is a bibliography for the study of painting and sculpture in Greece, Italy, France, Spain, Germany, England and Ireland. For literature too, his enthusiasm is obvious. William Butler Yeats (whose work he did not like), James Joyce, John Millington Synge and Dean Swift dominate the domestic scene, while Sir Walter Scott, Jane Austen, W. H. Auden, Stephen Spender and Virginia Woolf are cross-channel-born writers mainly featured in his notes. But his literary interests were universal and so we find French authors like Rimbaud, Voltaire, Rabelais, Gide, Proust and Zola noted alongside snippets on Chinese and Japanese literature. Gorki, Tolstoy and Chekhov lead his Russian section. Norwegian novels find mention and the classical Latin works of Catullus and Horace are not excluded. His period in New Mexico is reflected by notes on its literature.

French culture and Celtic civilisation are featured topics, as well as the ancient cultures of Peking and Peru. French architecture finds his approval:

> Back again in Toulouse with its brick architecture which I like so much, but I have little time as the mountains are not very far away and I must be off.

'I must be off.' The incessant traveller's fascination with church architecture is mirrored in observations on sepulchres, spires and minarets as far flung as Wexford, Clonmacnoise, Barcelona and New York.

An examination of the art of dance in Russia appears alongside a discussion on American ballads and Negro music. Coupled with comment on Spanish and English chamber music, these suggest a universality in taste.

He found time to dwell on philosophy too. Hegel, Spengler and Spinoza were subjects for his musings.

Lord Killanin recalled that he had a passion for photographing items of archaeological value, often spending long, exhausting periods of time awaiting proper lighting conditions for his work.

Ernie compiled reports on systems of education within the United States including the 'Dalton Plan'. Mainly, these were taken from *The New Republic, The Nation* and *Freeman*. He held texts for Mexican students published by the Mexican Secretariat of Education. From these and other journals on psychology, he culled portraits of Carl Gustav Jung, who formulated a system of analytical psychology, and his mentor Sigmund Freud, the founder of psychoanalysis. Their approach to the study of human personality involved the rigorous probing of the individual's motives, goals and attitudes to life. It appears to have appealed to Ernie.

Assorted programmes of events from Ernie's collection include the tenth season of the Irish Film Society (1945-46) in the Theatre-de-Luxe, the summer meetings of the Royal Society of Antiquarians (1950), a talk on mediaeval sculpture in Ireland at the Thomond Archaeological Society, the Payne School of Mime and Dance at Father Matthew Hall in November 1937 — these mix uneasily with the Killinick Harriers Point-to-Point and the Lenten address at New York's Riverside Church.

There was a toast to The King, The College, The Guests and The (College) Historical Society at that organisation's 150th Session Christmas Dinner in Trinity Dining Hall on 3 June 1920. Its programme lies alongside one for a function at the Gresham Hotel, Dublin, on 1 June 1946, when a presentation was made to Comdt Tom Byrne, last serving officer of the Irish Brigade in the Boer War.

Among Ernie O'Malley's unpublished material is a substantial manuscript biography of Seán Connolly, the Longford leader in the War of Independence who gave his name to the army barracks in the town. The longhand appears on assorted stationery. Some bear the official harp crest. Emblazoned on other sheets is EASTERN STATES ASSOCIATION OF PROFESSIONAL SCHOOLS FOR TEACHERS, Room 33, Press Buildings, Washington Square East, New York. American Promotion Committee also appears, indicating that some of the Connolly story was written during his period in the United States.

Ever encouraging to young people, Ernie advised them to read Shakespeare and the metaphysical John Donne as well as Spender's and Auden's work of social protest. He once referred to writing as his own only ethical code as he warned a young friend to show her work only to other writers, not to become a 'tea-house' writer reading stories to people who think the work wonderful.

Remaining quiet, he advised, was better.

That he heeded his own advice was apparent when he spent long and strict hours at the Yaddo Foundation preparing his book. Afterwards, in New York, he preferred heavy participation in intellectual and cultural pursuits to the city's sparkling social life.

He did not use the aura of authorship to while away lazy hours at bar counters. This was in contrast to the accepted norm in Irish literary circles.

# 7

# Envoy

*There's many a fearless rebel*
*In Westport and Clew Bay*
*Who watch with longing eagerness*
*For Freedom's dawning day.*

The Ernie O'Malley story is not ended. In 1978 Helen Hooker O'Malley Roelofs conveyed to the government of Ireland her desire to make an appropriate gift, in Ernie's memory, to the people of the west of Ireland, for whom she had great respect.

Over 600 works of art, valued at over $300,000 dollars, were involved. These included paintings, sculptures, oriental and south-eastern Asian objects, North American Indian items, photographs, stained glass, ceramics, metals, textiles, costumes and rugs.

Paul Henry, Evie Hone, Louis de Brocquy, Seán O'Sullivan, Jack Yeats (painting); Oisin Kelly, Brigid Rynn, Michael O'Sullivan (sculpture) — Irish names were as impressive as those from all over the world. This was to be but a beginning. The 'O'Malley Loan Collection' was not to become a static memorial.

Primarily educational (there was a stipulation about opening on school holidays), the Castlebar museum was to become a source of inspiration and knowledge for generations of young people in the west — as well as a worthwhile tourist amenity. The donor understood what sparked creativity and this was her main concern. She wisely avoided trying to vie with larger museums and galleries and envisaged a collection of physical beauty rather than an academic presentation. She was also to provide for additions in the future.

All Mayo appeared to be engrossed in preparations for

the Pope's visit to Knock when negotiations with Mrs
Roelofs and Cormac O'Malley were taking place. Yet
rapid progress was made in the acquisition of a site; the
county manager Michael O'Malley and county secretary
Mr John O'Donnell showing credit-worthy enthusiasm.

Helen wished particularly that a new building should be
built in a prominent position within Ernie's home town of
Castlebar. The Department of Education deemed the project to fall within the school-related financing programme.
It would, therefore, come under the control of the Voca-
tional Education Committee. Helen impressed some
Castlebar administrators by her sense of purpose and her
desire to help the community into which Ernie was born.
Some tireless efforts were made to bring about the transfer
of a suitable site to the VEC for a nominal sum. The site,
facing onto the corner of the Green, Castlebar, was
immediately available.

On 30 November 1979, interested parties met and a considerable amount of agreement was reached. The attendance included Mrs Helen O'Malley Roelofs, Cormac
O'Malley, deputies, county councillors, Department of
Education representatives, the county education officer
and county architect. The Irish-American Cultural
Institute had an interest, so three of their members with
four elected members of the VEC, two from the Department of Education, one from Castlebar UDC and two from
Mayo County Council were to form a management committee.

The local press was forecasting that the complex would
be completed within two years. But the *Western Journal*
reported: MAYO COULD LOSE O'MALLEY TREASURES
while the Newport based *Mayo News* waded in with: CRUX
OVER SITING OF O'MALLEY MUSEUM — and included an
offer to build it in Newport! Ballina offered to accommo-
date the collection too.

In 1982, no start had been made on the project. Was a
generous and imaginative gesture spiked on the railings of
bureaucracy or was an initial enthusiasm for a prestigious
concept deflated by apathetic tacks on the road to

accomplishment? A preliminary investigation did not reveal any clear reason. However, there did appear to exist a delicate situation which would be better left unexplored. The very possibility of such a laudable enterprise demanded that every care should be taken to avoid any controversy which might adversely affect its fruition.

Let the Ernie O'Malley Story close with the hope that the museum intended to perpetuate his memory, his wife's dream, will not go the way of Ernie's own life's dream by remaining incomplete.

# Index

Wexford, 52, 117
White, James, 116
Wicklow, 52
Willis, Dick, 36, 37
Wills Moody, Helen, 89
Wilson, Field Marshal Sir Henry,
  48, 80
Woods, Tony, 7, 100, 103, 104, 112

World War, First, 33, 49
World War, Second, 99
*Workers' Republic,* 15

Yaddo, 88, 119
Yeats, Jack B., 101, 116, 120
Yeats, W. B., 102, 117
Young, Ella, 75, 76, 79